been largely replaced by benzodiazepines, a class of drugs with a higher therapeutic index and lesser side effects. Barbiturates are still used to treat seizures, migraine headaches, and to induce anesthesia in surgical procedures. Typical barbiturates that are used are pentobarbital, amobarbital, secobarbital and phenobarbital. The Department of Defense discontinued testing for barbiturates in 2005 for the military drug testing program because prevalence of use was low. Barbiturates are classified as ultra-short acting, short-acting and intermediate-acting. Barbiturates are administered both orally and intravenously with high bioavailability. Barbiturates are metabolized via oxidation followed by conjugation and primary excretion in urine [17].

Initial screening for the presence of barbiturates in urine specimens is carried out using various immunoassays and is very reliable for this purpose. These immunoassays are usually calibrated with secobarbital but demonstrate significant cross-reactivities with other barbiturates. Confirmation testing for barbiturates is most commonly performed using GC–MS analysis following either liquid/liquid or solid phase extraction. Liquid/liquid extraction is performed at an acidic/neutral pH with small volumes of specimens. Solid phase extraction can be performed using silica based and copolymer based columns. Alkylation is the most common derivatization technique used for barbiturates to allow for improved chromatography and deuterated barbiturates are used as internal standards. Methylation of barbiturates can be easily carried out using iodomethane/tetramethylammonium hydroxide in dimethylsulfoxide. The deuterated pentobarbital (pentobarbital-d_5) can be used as the internal standard [18]. In Fig. 3.3 the total ion chromatogram for methylated barbiturates is given to show resolution of various barbiturates by capillary column.

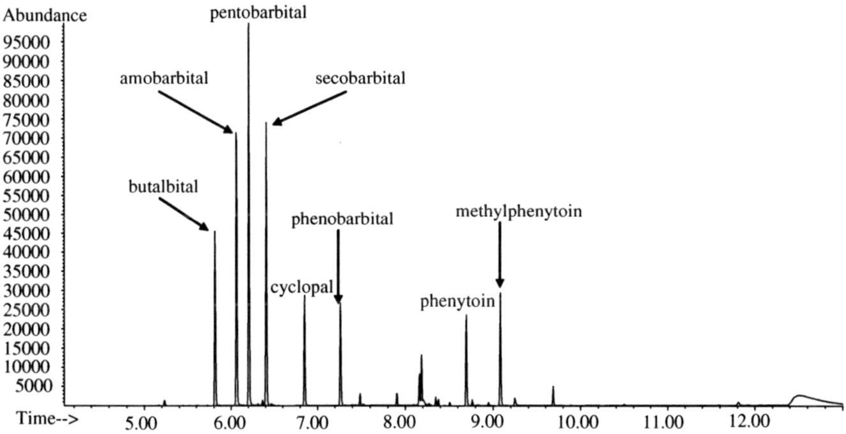

Fig. 3.3 GC–MS total ion chromatogram for methylated barbiturates at 2 mg/L in blood. Figure courtesy of Dr. Buddha D. Paul, Office of the Armed Forces Medical Examiner (OAFME), Forensic Toxicology Division of the Armed Forces Institute of Pathology, Rockville, MD

4.2 Testing of Benzodiazepines

For commercially available immunoassays the target analyte is typically oxazepam or nordiazepam. The disadvantage of most benzodiazepine immunoassays is that they are designed to cross react with unconjugated drugs. The addition of β-glucuronidase to the screening reagent will allow for enzymatic hydrolysis prior to analytical measurement by cleaving the glucuronide conjugated metabolites, thus improving sensitivity [19]. Flunitrazepam (Rohypnol®) is a benzodiazepine which is not legally available in the United States. However, this drug is found on the clandestine market and is widely abused in the United States and is also associated with date rape situations. One of the major metabolite of flunitrazepam is 7-aminoflunitrazepam which cross-reacts with antibodies used in the benzodiazepine screening assays. For example, cross-reactivity of 7-aminoflunitrazepam with EMIT Plus assay is 67.8%, and the corresponding cross-reactivity with CEDIA assay is 99%. Unfortunately, due to low concentrations of flunitrazepam and its major metabolite 7-aminoflunitrazepam, an immunoassay for benzodiazepine may fail to detect the presence of flunitrazepam in urine. There are commercially available immunoassays on the market, for example, a specific enzyme-linked immunosorbent assay marketed by Cozart Bioscience Ltd (Oxfordshire, UK) for the screening of flunitrazepam in urine [20].

For GC/MS confirmation, benzodiazepines can be extracted from biological specimens by either liquid/liquid or solid-phase extraction. Prior to extraction of urine specimens, a hydrolysis step must be completed to cleave the glucuronide conjugation. Most procedures use an enzymatic hydrolysis because it is a weaker reaction than acid hydrolysis which can convert some benzodiazepines to benzophenones. Adjustment of pH following hydrolysis is necessary for both extraction techniques. Derivatization is not required for some benzodiazepines such as diazepam and midazolam but it is necessary for others, including 7-aminoclonazepam and α-hydroxyalprazolam. Popular derivative choices are alkyl, acyl, and silyl derivatives.

4.3 Testing of Methadone

Methadone is metabolized to two pharmacologically inactive urinary metabolites, 2-ethylidene-1,5-dimethyl-3,3-diphenylpyrrolidine (EDDP) and 2-ethyl-5-methyl-3,3-diphenylpyrrolidine (EMDP). Usually both methadone and EDDP are found in urine in significant amounts while the concentration of EDMP is relatively low. Cheng et al. reported that urinary methadone concentration varied from 78 to 9,547 ng/mL (median: 1,031 ng/mL) and EDDP concentration varied from 77 to 9,547 ng/mL (median: 6,734 ng/mL) in 21 urine specimens collected from patients undergoing methadone maintenance therapy. The concentrations of EMDP were below the detection limit of the GC/MS assay [21]. Commercially available immunoassays for screening of methadone in urine have antibodies either directed towards methadone or EDDP. However, an immunoassay designed for detecting the presence of methadone in urine may have a low cross-reactivity with EDDP.

4.4 Testing of Propoxyphene

Propoxyphene is used for treating mild to moderate pain but this drug is also abused. Both propoxyphene and its metabolite nor-propoxyphene can be observed in urine and in most immunoassays the target analyte is propoxyphene. The cross-reactivity of the antibody with nor-propoxyphene may vary widely between different immunoassays. McNally et al. concluded that the ONLINE propoxyphene assay (Roche Diagnostics, Indianapolis, IN) has better sensitivity that the EMIT propoxyphene assay for detecting the presence of propoxyphene in urine because the antibody used in the ONLINE assay has 77% cross-reactivity with nor-propoxyphene while the EMIT assay has only 7% cross-reactivity with nor-propoxyphene [22]. Diphenhydramine (Benadryl®) interferes with the EMIT propoxyphene immunoassay [23]. The confirmation of the presence of propoxyphene in urine should be carried out by GC/MS and the assay should be able to determine the concentration of both propoxyphene and its major metabolite nor-propoxyphene.

4.5 Testing of Methaqualone and Glutethimide

Methaqualone is metabolized to 2′-hydroxy and 3′-hydroxy metabolites which are then conjugated and excreted in urine as glucuronide. Brenner et al. reported that both Roche ONLINE methaqualone immunoassay and EMIT II methaqualone immunoassay have high cross reactivity toward both 2- and 3-hydroxy metabolites of methaqualone as well as their conjugated form and are useful for screening of methaqualone in urine specimens. When volunteers received 200 mg of methaqualone, both immunoassays showed greater than 600 ng/mL of drug after the second void and all urine specimens tested highly positive (at a 300 ng/mL cut-off) for 72 h. When the specimens were analyzed by GC/MS without hydrolysis of glucuronide conjugates, low levels of methaqualone and metabolites were detected. However, when urine specimens were hydrolyzed with beta-glucuronidase and then analyzed again by GC/MS, high concentrations of metabolites were found. Therefore authors recommend hydrolysis of the urine specimen prior to GC/MS analysis [24].

Glutethimide, a sedative, is also abused. It undergoes complex metabolism into several metabolites and some metabolites such as 4-hydroxygluthemide and 2-phenylglutarimide have significant pharmacological activities. Immunoassays can be used for screening for the presence of glutethimide in urine. GC/MS confirmation is also capable of confirming the presence of metabolites along with the parent drug in urine. However, only less than 2% of glutethimide is excreted unchanged in urine.

5 Miscellaneous Issues in Workplace Drug Testing

Immunoassay positive test results are considered as presumptive positive and such results must be confirmed by GC/MS in workplace drug testing. The major limitation of immunoassays is the cross-reactivity from structurally related compounds while GC/MS confirmation is free from such limitations (except that optical isomers can be resolved). However, using special derivatization method using chiral derivatization agents, even optical isomers can be analyzed by GC/MS. There are many examples of limitations of immunoassays. For example, amphetamine immunoassays are mostly affected because a number of structurally similar compounds such as buflomedil, brompheniramine, chlorpromazine, ephedrine, fenfluramine, isometheptene, mexiletine, *N*-acetyl procainamide (metabolite of procainamide), perazine, phenmetrazine, phentermine, phenylpropanolamine, promethazine, pseudoephedrine, quinacrine, ranitidine, tolmetin and tyramine are known to cross-react with various amphetamine assays causing false positive results [25–27]. Dietzen et al. demonstrated that urine specimens containing ranitidine greater than 43 μg/mL interferes with Beckman Synchron amphetamine, but other Beckman assays such as opiate, barbiturates, cocaine metabolite, propoxyphene and methadone have good specificity while the cannabinoid assay has 100% predictive value based on GC/MS confirmation [28]. Tolmetin, a non-steroidal antiinflammatory drug, can interfere with EMIT assays for urine drug screening if the drug is present in a significant amount (1,800 mg/L). Tolmetin has characteristic high molar absorbance at 340 nm which is the wavelength for detection of signal in EMIT assays. A specimen collected from an arthritic patient receiving 100–400 mg tolmetin showed decreased signal when mixed with abused drugs and analyzed by EMIT assays. Similar interference of tolmetin in FPIA assays for drugs of abuse was not observed because a different wavelength (525 nm) is used for detecting signals. However, potential false positive test results using FPIA benzodiazepine assay were observed when urine specimens contained high concentrations of fenoprofen, flurbiprofen, indomethacin, ketoprofen and also tolmetin [29].

If a specimen is tested positive by the immunoassay and tested negative by GC/MS, the specimen is reported as "negative." If a urine specimen is tested positive, the MRO (medical review officer) must determine that the person is abusing drugs and there is no alternate explanation of analytical positive specimen. There are multiple mechanisms such as chain of custody, review by MRO, etc. which are implemented in workplace drug testing to ensure that an innocent person is not falsely penalized.

6 Conclusions

In workplace drug testing, measures are taken to ensure accuracy of the result and, for this purpose, specimen collection process, transportation of specimens to the laboratory, analysis of specimens and reporting of results are all important. The goal is to identify employees who are abusing drugs on a regular basis. Immunoassays are used as the initial screening tool but positive results must be confirmed by GC/MS or another acceptable robust analytical technique.

References

1. Ricordel I, Wenzek M. Cannabis and safety work: evolution of its detection within the controls of narcotics since 2004 to the SNCF. Ann Pharm Fr 2008; 66: 255–260.
2. Roberts S, Fallon LF Jr. Administrative issues related to addiction in the workplace. Occup Med 2001; 16: 509 515.
3. Bush DM. The US mandatory guidelines for federal workplace drug testing programs: current status and future considerations. Forensic Sci Int 2008; 174: 111–119.
4. Dackis CA, Pottash AJC, Annitto W, Gold MS. Persistence of marijuana level after supervised abstinence. Am J Psychiatry 1982; 139: 1196–1198.
5. Huestis MA, Mitchell JM, Cone EJ. Detection time of marijuana metabolite in urine by immunoassays and GC–MS. J Anal Toxicol 1995; 19: 443–449.
6. Huestis MA, Darwin WD, Shimoura E, Lalani SA et al. Cocaine and metabolites urinary excretion after controlled smoke administration. J Anal Toxicol 2007; 31: 462–468.
7. Moeller KE, Lee KC, Kissack JC. Urine drug screen: practical guides for clinicians. Mayo Clin Proc 2008; 83: 66–76.
8. Loor R, Lingerfelter C, Wason PP, Tank K et al. Multiplex assay of amphetamine, methamphetamine, and ecstasy drug using CEDIA technology. J Anal Toxicol 2002; 26: 267–273.
9. Lekskulchai V, Mokkhavesa C. Evaluation of Roche Abuscreen ONLINE amphetamine immunoassay for screening of new amphetamine analogs. J Anal Toxicol 2001; 25: 471–475.
10. McGilveray IJ. Pharmacokinetics of cannabinoids. Pain Res Manag 2005; 10(A): 15A–22A.
11. Fraser AD, Worth D. Urinary excretion of 11-nor-9-carboxy-delta9-tetrahydrocannaninol and 11-hydroxy-delta9-THC: cannabinoid metabolites to creatinine ratio stuffy IV. Forensic Sci Int 2004; 143: 147–152.
12. Goodwin RS, Darwin WD, Chiang CN, Shih M et al. Urinary elimination of 11-nor-9-cerboxy-delta 9-tetrahydrocannabinol in cannabis users during continuously monitored abstinence. J Anal Toxicol 2008; 32: 562–569.
13. Joern WA. Detection of past and recurrent marijuana use by a modified GC/MS procedure. J Anal Toxicol 1987; 11: 49–52.
14. Cone EJ, Tsadik A, Oyler J, Darwin WD. Cocaine metabolism and urinary excretion after different routes of administration. Ther Drug Monit 1998; 20: 556–560.
15. Wu AH, Ostheimer D, Cremese M, Forte E et al. Characterization of drug interference caused by coelution of substances in gas chromatography/mass spectrometry confirmation of targeted drugs in full scan and selected ion monitoring modes. Clin Chem 1994; 40: 216–220.
16. Dasgupta A, Mahle C, McLemore J. Elimination of fluconazole interference in gas chromatography/mass spectrometric confirmation of benzoylecgonine, the major metabolite of cocaine using pentafluropropionyl derivative. J Foresnsic Sci 1996; 41: 511–513.
17. Jenkins AJ, Cone EJ. Pharmacokinetics: Drug absorption, distribution, and elimination. In: SB Karch ed. Drug Abuse Handbook. CRC Press, Washington, D.C., 1998, pp. 151–201.
18. Liu RH, McKeehan AM, Edwards C, Foster G et al. Improved gas chromatography/mass spectrometric analysis of barbiturates in urine using centrifuge-based solid phase extraction, methylation with d-5 pentobarbital as internal standard. J Forensic Sci 1994; 39: 1504–1514.
19. Klette KL. Urine benzodiazepine screening using Roche Online® KIMS immunoassay with β-glucuronidase hydrolysis and confirmation by gas chromatography – mass spectrometry. J Anal Toxicol 2005; 29: 193–200.

20. Wang PH, Liu C, Tsay WI et al.. Improved screen and confirmation test of 7-aminoflunitrazepam in urine specimens for monitoring flunitrazepam (Rohypnol) in urine. J Anal Toxicol 2002; 26: 411–418.
21. Cheng PS, Lee CH, Liu C, Chen CS. Simultaneous determination of Ketamine, Tramadol, Methadone and their metabolites in urine by gas chromatography-mass spectrometry. J Anal Toxicol 2008; 32: 253–259.
22. McNally AJ, Pilcher I, Wu R, Salamone SJ et al. Evaluation of the online immunoassay for propoxyphene: comparison to EMIT II and GC–MS. J Anal Toxicol 1996; 20: 537–540.
23. Schneider S, Wennig R. Interference of diphenhydramine with the EMIT II immunoassay for propoxyphene. J Anal Toxicol 1999; 23: 637–638.
24. Brenner C, Hui R, Passarelli J, Wu R et al. Comparison of methaqualone excretion patterns using Abuscreen ONLINE and EMIT II immunoassay and GC/MS. Forensic Sci Int 1996; 79: 31–41.
25. Moore KA. Amphetamines/sympathomimetic amines. In: Levine B ed. Principles of Forensic Toxicology. AACC Press, Washington, D.C, 2003, pp. 341–348.
26. Grinstead GF. Ranitidine and high concentration phenylpropanolamine cross react in the EMIT monoclonal amphetamine/methamphetamine assay. Clin Chem 1989; 35: 1998–1999.
27. Joseph R, Dickerson S, Wills R, Frankenfield D et al. Interference by non-steroidal antiinflammatory drugs in EMIT and TDX assays for drugs of abuse. J Anal Toxicol 1995; 19: 13–17.
28. Dietzen DJ, Ecos K, Friedman D, Beason S. Positive predictive values of abused drug immunoassay on the Beckman Synchron in a veteran population. J Anal Toxicol 2001; 25: 174–178.
29. Joseph R, Dickerson S, Willis R, Frankenfield D et al. Interference by nonsteroidal anti-inflammatory drugs in EMIT and TDx assays for drugs of abuse. J Anal Toxicol 1995; 19: 13–17.

Chapter 4
Synthetic Urine, Flushing, Detoxifying, and Related Agents for Beating Urine Drug Tests: Are They Effective?

Abstract Searching the Internet with key words Beat + Drug Test produced over 140,000 results, indicating that many commercial products are readily available through the Internet for the purpose of invalidating urine drug testing. Fortunately, most of the products have no documented ability to invalidate drug tests and may be considered mostly as an advertising gimmick. although synthetic urine has characteristic properties of normal urine, a simple temperature check at the point of collection may provide a clue to identify such specimens. In addition, diuretics such as hydrochlorothiazide as well as various detoxifying agents may produce dilute urine where the creatinine concentration may be below an acceptable limit. Contrary to the claims of the manufacturers, these detoxifying agents and herbal pills are mostly ineffective in invalidating a urine drugs test result.

Keywords Detoxifying agents · Flushing agents · Synthetic urine

1 Introduction

Commercially available products to beat drug tests can be divided into two major categories: (1) products that are often taken orally to flush out unwanted drugs and toxins from the body, and (2) adulterants which are added to urine specimen after collection in order to invalidate drug testing. In addition, synthetic urine specimens are also available from various Internet sites. Synthetic urine has all normal characteristics of normal human urine and persons undergoing workplace drug testing attempt to substitute this synthetic urine as their specimen. In addition, a person may ingest diuretic medication with a hope of producing dilute urine where concentrations of abused drug or metabolite may be below the cut-off concentration of the screening assay. For example, the cut-off concentration of benzoylecgonine (metabolite of cocaine) in the immunoassay screening step is 300 ng/mL. Therefore, if the concentration of benzoylecgonine is below 300 ng/mL the specimen is considered negative. If a person has abused cocaine a few days prior to drug testing and may have a concentration just over the cut-off, and the individual drinks plenty of

DOI 10.1007/978-1-60761-527-9_4,

water and a diuretic medication or a detoxifying agents which usually contains caffeine, a diuretic, the urine specimen will be diluted, thus pushing the concentration below the screening cut-off of 300 ng/mL. If a specimen is tested negative by the immunoassays, it usually does not undergo further analysis by a more sophisticated and specific confirmation technique such as gas chromatography/mass spectrometry, and thus the individual may pass the drug test. In reality, these approaches are not very effective in beating a workplace urine drug test.

2 Synthetic Urine

In general, many Internet sites appear to sell the same synthetic urine product and it costs between $31 to over $100. Quick Fix synthetic urine is available from an Internet site (http://www.ddetox.com/products_1939html) for $31.99. Another Internet site (http://detoxland.com) also sells this product for $31.99 and yet another (http://www.boxdetox.com) for $31.99. The Quick Fix container can be microwaved for 10 s for initial heating with the cap open to achieve a temperature between 94 and 100°F, which is the expected temperature range of normal urine after collection. A heater pad is also provided with the Quick Fix synthetic urine which should also be heated with the urine and then should be taped to the urine specimen with the cap closed. The manufacturer claims that synthetic urine can maintain the desired temperature if taped with the heating pad for up to 6 h in an inside pocket of clothing being worn.

Ultra pure premixed synthetic urine is available from Detox.com (http://www.detoxshops.com) for $31.99. A 4-oz size of ultra pure synthetic urine costs $41.99, while this site also sells Quick Fix synthetic urine for $31.99. A 4-oz size of ultra pure synthetic urine is also sold for $41.99 from another Internet site which sells various products to cheat on a drug test (http://www.boxdetox.com). Tinkle brand synthetic urine is sold by the Internet site http://www.syntheticurine.com, and is a pre-mixed liquid packaged in a 2-oz plastic container along with a heat temperature strip and a hand warmer. The Internet site says that this product cannot be shipped in seven states (AK, IL, KY, OK, NJ, NC and SC). The Internet site http://www.cleartest.com/products/synthetic-urine also sells synthetic urine for $35.99. This synthetic urine is available in concentrated form and should be mixed with warm water at body temperature to produce a urine specimen that should be submitted for drug testing in order to pass a drug test. The kit comes with two vials containing synthetic urine (enough for two tests), a plastic 4-oz bottle, two hand warmers and a temperature strip. The synthetic urine should be prepared by mixing concentrated urine with warm water (including tap water) and then the temperature strip should be used to check the temperature of the specimen to ensure that it is within the acceptable limit. The manufacturer recommends that body temperature of the specimen is maintained by putting it under armpits or alternatively in pants. In addition, the manufacturer also sells a device called "Urinator" which is a small electronic device that maintains temperature of the synthetic urine specimen at body temperature for up to 4 h. This device is battery operated (two 9-V batteries) and is sold for $149.95.

Human urine specimens not containing any drugs (frozen urine or dehydrated urine) are also available for substitution purposes in order to beat a drug test. Fortunately, in many States like South Carolina, North Carolina, Nebraska, New Jersey, etc. it is illegal to sell or give away urine for the purpose of defrauding a drug test. In South Carolina one person was selling his urine for $69 per sample in order to pass the drug test. The person was arrested and found guilty by the Supreme Court of South Carolina. Unfortunately, if substituted urine specimen cannot be identified by temperature index at the collection site, there is no way to identify substituted urine by any laboratory test.

3 Composition of Synthetic Urine

The composition of normal human urine varies widely from one individual to another because of the difference in fluid intake, diet, presence of any disease such as diabetes and various other factors. In general, normal human urine is composed of both organic compounds and inorganic salt. Usually urea and creatinine are the major organic compounds in urine along with uric acid. In addition, very small amounts of protein, fatty acid, hormones and a variety of other organic products are found in urine. Inorganic cations found in urine include sodium, potassium, chloride, magnesium, and calcium while inorganic anions are ammonium, sulphate and various phosphates. The pH of normal human urine may vary widely between acidic and basic. The pH of normal urine varies within the same day but should be within 4.5–8.0. The specific gravity should be between 1.005 and 1.030. The creatinine concentration of normal urine varies between 20 and 400 mg/dL. Synthetic urine mimics these values. However, certain trace macromolecules which are normally found in urine specimens may not be present in synthetic urine. There are various formulas for preparing synthetic urine for research. Mayrovitz and Sims dissolved 25 g of urea, 2 g of creatinine, 9 g of sodium chloride, 2.5 g of disodium hydrogen orthophosphate anhydrous, 3 g of ammonium chloride, and 3 g of sodium sulphite hydrated in 1 L of water to prepared synthetic urine for their study. The pH of the synthetic urine was adjusted to 7.8 [1].

In general, synthetic urine has the same specific gravity, pH and creatinine content as expected in a normal urine specimen. The color of normal urine is due to pigments known as urochromes. Artificial color can be added to synthetic urine to mimic the color of normal urine. Synthetic urine cannot be distinguished from normal urine by specimen integrity testing except for careful visual inspection.

4 Specimen Integrity Testing

Both the collection site and the laboratory have a number of mechanisms to detect adulterated specimens. The temperature of urine specimen should be checked within 4 min of collection and the temperature should be between 32 and 38°C (90–100.4°F) but urine specimens may remain warmer than 33°C for up to 15 min.

The pH of normal urine varies within the same day but should be within 4.5–8.0. The specific gravity should be between 1.005 and 1.030. The creatinine concentration of normal urine varies between 20 and 400 mg/dL. A specimen is considered as diluted if the creatinine is <20 mg/dL and the specific gravity is less than 1.003. Additional tests are also recommended to detect the presence of other adulterants. Determination of specific gravity is mandatory for any specimen with a creatinine concentration of less than 20 mg/dL. Although substituted urine should have a normal creatinine concentration, specific gravity and pH, the temperature may not be within the acceptable limit if the person being tested did not carefully heat the synthetic or substituted specimen to achieve the desired temperature or failed to maintain the desired temperature of the urine while traveling to the testing facility. This may be apparent in a cold climate where the individual might have walked several blocks from a parking spot. Another important feature of identifying synthetic urine is visual inspection of the specimen. Sometimes contents of synthetic urine settle down in the form of a precipitate if it is not vigorously shaken prior to submitting as a specimen. Observing floating objects in the urine specimen or sedimentation may also provide a clue that the specimen is not an authentic urine specimen.

Although the criteria described above are widely accepted by many clinical drug testing facilities, urine pH may be outside the limit of acceptability in unadulterated specimens if stored for a long time at elevated temperature. Cook et al. reported that several unadulterated urine specimens had a pH between 9.1 and 9.3. Although pH of a urine specimen is stable if stored at –20°C, storage at room temperature or higher may produce a pH above 9 but under no circumstances over 9.5. Degradation of nitrogenous compounds of the urine is most likely responsible for this phenomenon [2].

5 Prosthetic Penis and Workplace Drug Testing

In most workplace drug testing where urine specimen collection is not watched, a possibility that a person may substitute his or her urine with a synthetic or drug free urine always exists. In military and some other drug testing programs, the specimen collection process is supervised. Nevertheless, people still try to substitute urine specimen using several innovative ways. People use a life like prosthetic penis called "Whizzinator" and other related products to substitute urine specimens in order to cheat drug testing. The device which was sold by "Punk Technology" came with a complete pack of dried urine, heater pack to heat urine and a realistic prosthetic penis which comes in several skin tones such as white, tan, brown and black.

United States Attorney Mary Beth Buchanan announced on November 24, 2008 that George W. Wills, age 65, of San Padro, California, Robert Dennis Catalano, age 62, of Huntington Beach, California, and Puck Technology, Inc., a national Internet business located in Signal Hill, California, had each pleaded guilty to two counts before United States District Judge David Cercone. From October 10,

2005 through May 7, 2008, Wills and Catalano, using Puck Technology, conspired to defraud the Substance Abuse and Mental Health Services Administration (SAMHSA) of the United States Department of Health and Human Services by defeating and obstructing the lawful governmental functions of SAMHSA in federal workplace drug testing programs. During the period mentioned, Wills and Catalano, using Puck Technology, sold over the Internet sites, www.whizzinator.com and www.gonumber1.com, the product, the Whizzinator, a male prosthetic urinating device, and the product, Number 1, a urinating device made for both men and women, to customers throughout the United States and in the Western District of Pennsylvania, for the purpose of defeating federal, and federally regulated, employment drug urine tests overseen by SAMHSA for marijuana, cocaine and other controlled substances under Title 21 of the United States Code. The defendants and Puck Technology also sold on these websites synthetic urine to be used in these products, to be passed off as a customer's real urine at the time of the administration of a drug test, including those drug tests overseen by SAMHSA and conducted under federal law. Judge David Cercone scheduled sentencing for Wills and Catalano on February 20, 2009, at 11:00 a.m. and 11:30 a.m., respectively. The law provides for a maximum total sentence of 8 years in prison, a fine of $500,000, or both, for each defendant [3].

Although the owners of this company are in jail, other similar products may still be available on the market. Executive ultra realistic kit sold by http://www.ureaSample.com Internet site has the following devices:

1. One five inch ultra realistic prosthetic penis (available in three skin color tones)
2. Odor proof miniaturized transport system
3. Three foot tubing with dispenser allowing for placement of the transporter anywhere on the body
4. Two straps for attachment
5. Reusable self-adhesive thermometer strip to check temperature of the fake urine
6. Two 10-h chemical heat pads
7. Plastic syringe, latex gloves and instruction booklet

Again the use of such devices create a serious problem in workplace drug testing unless synthetic urine delivered can be identified by a slight difference in expected temperature or observing other physical characteristics. If these specimens cannot be identified in the pre-analytical state, a person may successfully beat a workplace drug testing.

5.1 Catheterization for Substituting Urine

A dangerous procedure for a drug addict is to void and then insert a catheter to reach the bladder followed by injecting clean synthetic urine or clean urine into the bladder. Both males and females attempt to cheat drug testing using catheterization especially if the collection process is supervised. Although effective in cheating a drug test, use of a non-sterilized thin plastic tube instead of a medically sterilized catheter may cause severe infection in the urinary tract. Even hospitalized patients where a catheter is placed under medical supervision are known to get an infection from the use of a catheter. In addition, people try to conceal clean urine in a condom or a container and tape the specimen to the thigh or any other parts of the body in order to cheat on a workplace drug testing. A woman may attempt to conceal a condom full of clean urine in her vagina.

6 Flushing and Detoxifying Products

There are many flushing and detoxifying products available through various Internet sites. These products must be ingested following written instructions and all such products encourage the person attempting to beat drug tests to drink lots of fluids and water. The goal is to produce diluted urine so that concentration of a drug or its metabolite can be pushed below the cut-off concentration of the screening immunoassay. This approach may be helpful if the drug concentration is relatively low in the body but ineffective for a heavy drug abuser.

The costs of detoxifying products vary widely depending on the type of detoxifying desired and also on the Internet sites from which they are available. From the Internet site (http://www.passyourdrugtest1.com) 7-day detoxifying products designed for people over 180 lb and heavy users of drugs are sold for $109.95. The 5-day detoxifying formula designed for heavy to moderate users with body weight 180 lb or less costs $79.95 and comes with two drug testing options. Another Internet site (http://www.testpassed.com) sells premium detox 7-day comprehensive cleansing program for $59.99 and also sells THC/marijuana cannabis dip strip urine drug testing for $3.99. The fast THC/marijuana detox kit for people under 200 lb is sold for $51.99 while the two step THC/marijuana detox kit for people under 200 lb is sold for $45.99. The fast cocaine detox kit for people over 200 lb is sold for $55.99. The same site also sells cheaper products such as Absolute De-Tox carbo Drink, Grape Flavor for $34.99, ZYDOT Natural Blend Cleansing Tea for $19.99, Flax Boost for 19.99, Detoxifying Quick Flash capsules for $24.99, etc. The Aqua Clean Cleansing system is also available from an Internet site (http://www.ddtox.com/product_2692.html) for $31.99. The site claims that dissolving two tablets in water and drinking the water will be effective 1 h before the scheduled drug testing and the effects last for up to 5 h. A variety of other products, for example, Absolute Detox XXL drink, Absolute Carbo Drinks, Ready Clean Drug Detox Drink, Fast Flush Capsules, Ready Clean Gel Capsules, etc. are all available from various Internet sites [4]. Many products are available from the Internet site http://detoxland.com for beating a drug test. Premium detox 7-day comprehensive program package is sold for 59.99, fast marijuana detox kit for people under 200 lb for $51.99 (for people over 200 lb this package is priced at $55.99), fast cocaine detox kit for people over 200 lb costs $55.99 and solution 4X is sold for $49.95. Super quick capsules for detoxification are also sold from the site at $25.99.

Another Internet site also sells detoxifying Quick Flush capsules for $24.99 and Aqua Clean cleansing system for $31.99 (http://www.eedru.com). Various flavors of Absolute Detox-Carbo drinks are available for prices between $31.99 and $39.99 from the Internet site http://boxdetox.com.

6.1 Water Intoxication

There are inherent dangers of drinking excessive water. Hyperhydration or water intoxication is a potentially fatal disturbance of brain function and electrolyte imbalance disease. Although death from water intoxication is rare in a healthy individual, a healthy person may die following drinking excessive water in a short period of time in water drinking contests or after exercise. Several reports during the past few years have described hyponatremia as a result of excessive water intake by athletes during endurance races. Interestingly, fatal water intoxication may also occur during urine specimen collection in urine drug testing.

Water intoxication in a patient is a valid cause of diluted urine specimen submitted for workplace drug testing. Finkel reported a case where a patient was evaluated medically after submitting a urine sample for drug screening that was considered inappropriately dilute. The medical evaluation revealed that the patient had chronic water intoxication from a very strict weight loss regime. Dietary solute intake may affect the water metabolism of the kidney, causing hyponatremia [5]. An army trainee developed acute water intoxication hyponatremia, pulmonary edema and fatal cerebral edema during a supervised excessive water ingestion in an attempt to induce sufficient urine specimen for drug testing. Following this incidence, the authors developed recommendation of limiting fluid intake to 8 oz every 30–45 min, not to exceed 40 oz and also to provide a relaxing reassuring environment to the person for obtaining a urine specimen [6]. Klonoff and Jurow reported an adverse consequence of workplace drug testing in a subject due to acute water intoxication and a literature review of seven other cases where water intoxication in patients was not related to psychiatric or neurologic illness. The authors concluded that, for workers undergoing urine drug testing, drinking 1 L of water and impaired urine dilution by the kidney are the risk factors for water intoxication producing unacceptably diluted urine. Symptoms of cerebral dysfunction should suggest the possibility of water intoxication in a recently drug tested person [7].

6.2 Diluted Urine and Drug Testing

Diluting urine is a simple way to make an otherwise positive drug test produce a negative result. Because this can be easily achieved by adding hot tap water to the urine specimen, most collection facilities do not have a hot tap water supply in the bathroom designed for specimen collection. In this case, if an individual dilutes the collected specimen using cold tap water, the temperature should fall well below the lower acceptable limit of urine specimens. Federal guidelines recommend placing a toilet bluing agent in the toilet tank if possible so that the reservoir of water in the toilet bowl always remains blue. Ideally, there should be no other source of water in the enclosure where urination takes place.

Consumption of a large amount of fluid prior to drug testing is a way to avoid a positive test by diluting the urine [8]. Usually a creatinine concentration below 20 mg/dL or a specific gravity below 1.003 may indicate diluted urine [9]. Jaffee et al. also considered a creatinine concentration below 20 mg/dL as a sign of diluted urine. In addition, an immunoglobulin (IgG) concentration below 0.5 μg/mL suggests either substitution or dilution [10]. Therefore, creatinine analysis is essential to determine whether the urine specimen is diluted. Needleman and Porvaznik considered a creatinine value of less than 10 mg/dL as suggestive of replacement of a urine specimen mostly by water [11].

Although most publications considered a creatinine concentration below 20 mg/dL (1.8 mmol/L), as the criteria of diluted urine, a few publications considered urine creatinine concentration below 45 mg/dL (4 mmol/L) as the criterion of diluted urine. Edwards et al. considered normal urine to have a creatinine concentration of above 45 mg/dL and specific gravity in the range 1.007–1.035 [12]. In another article, the authors suggested that urinary creatinine at <4 mmol/L (45 mg/dL) can be considered as a cut-off discriminating between physiologically and non-physiologically diluted urine. Following this approach, 100 urine specimens which tested negative for all drugs using initial immunoassay screening and had creatinine concentrations less than 4 mmol/L were evaporated at 37°C under a stream of nitrogen until creatinine concentration reached normal values (three- to sixfold concentrations). Using this approach, the mean creatinine value in these specimens increased from 2.74 mmol/L (31 mg/dL) to 9.91 mmol/L (112 mg/dL), and 14 negative specimens tested positive for morphine (cut-off 300 ng/mL), 1 specimen tested positive for cocaine (cut-off 300 ng/mL), 5 specimens tested positive for cannabinoids (cut-off 25 ng/mL), 5 specimens tested positive for benzodiazepines (cut-off 100 ng/mL) and 2 specimens tested positive for amphetamines (cut-off 200 ng/mL) [13].

The SAMHSA (Substance Abuse and Mental Health Services Administration of the Federal Government that provides guidelines for drug testing) program does not currently allow analysis of diluted urine specimens at lower screening and confirmation cut-offs than the recommended guidelines but in 2010 the agency recommends lowering both screening and confirmation cut-off of several drugs (see Chap. 3). In Canada, the Correctional Services of Canada (CSC) specimens incorporates lower screening and confirmation cut-off for drug/metabolites (amphetamine: screening cut-off 100 ng/mL, confirmation cut-off 100 ng/mL, benzoylecgonine: screening and confirmation cut-off 15 ng/mL, opiates, screening and confirmation cut-off 120 ng/mL, phencyclidine, screening and confirmation cut-off 5 ng/mL and cannabinoids, screening cut-off 20 ng/mL, confirmation cut-off 3 ng/mL) for diluted urine specimens. Fraser and Zamecnik reported that 7,912 urine specimens collected and analyzed between 2000 and 2002 by the CSC were dilute and, out of that, 26% screened positive using SAMSHA cut-off values. When lower values for cut-off and confirmation were adopted, 1,100 specimens tested positive for one or more illicit drugs. The positive rate of diluted specimens was 18.2% in CSC institutes and 22.3% in parolee specimens. The drug most often confirmed positive in a diluted specimen is marijuana. Codeine and/or morphine were also commonly confirmed in these urine specimens and ranked second after marijuana in prevalence [14]. Soldin reported that there was more than a 100% increase in cocaine positive specimens when the cut-off was lowered to 80 ng/mL from the recommended 300 ng/mL in a pediatric population because neonates are not capable of concentrating urine to the same extent as adults [15]. Luzzi et al. investigated the analytic performance criteria of three immunoassay systems (EMIT, Beckman EIA and Abbott FPIA) for detecting abused drugs below established cut-off values. The authors concluded that drugs can be screened at concentrations much lower than that established by SAMSHA cut-off values. For example, the authors proposed a THC–COOH cut-off value of 35 ng/mL using EMIT, and 14 ng/mL for the Beckman EIA, and the FPIA assay, where SAMSHA guidelines stated a cut-off value of 50 ng/mL. The proposed cut-off values were based on the studies of precision of the assays at proposed lower detection limit where the CV was less than 20%. This lowering of the cut-off values increased the number of positive specimens in the screening tests to 15.6%. A 7.8% increase was also observed in the confirmation stage of drugs of abuse testing [16].

6.3 SAMHSA Criteria for Diluted/Substituted Urine

In February 2000, the SAMHSA (under the United States Department of Health and Human Services) published the National Laboratory Certification Program (NLPL) State of Science – Update 1, entitled Urine Specimen Validity Testing: Evaluation of the Scientific Data Used to Define a Urine Specimen as "Substituted" [17]. A substituted specimen is defined as urine with a creatinine content less than or equal to 5 mg/dL and a specific gravity $\leq$1.001 or $\geq$1.020. In reality, such low values of creatinine and specific gravity are not physiologically possible to reach in normal human urine. Cook et al. concluded that creatinine equal to or less than 5 mg/dL and specific gravity equal to or less than 1.001 is not consistent with clinical characteristics of normal urine [18].

Edgell et al. performed a controlled hydration study using 56 normal volunteers to investigate whether it is possible to produce such diluted urine. Subjects were given 2,370 mL of fluid, and urine specimens were collected at the end of each hour for a 6-h test period. No urine specimen satisfied the paired substitution criteria (specific gravity $\leq$1.001 or above 1.020 and creatinine $\leq$5.0 mg/dL) for diluted urine although 55% of subjects produced at least one dilute urine specimen during the first 3 h of hydration with creatinine $<$20 mg/dL and specific gravity $<$1.003. This finding supports the criteria set by SAMSHA for classifying a specimen as substituted if creatinine is below 5 mg/dL and specific gravity $\leq$1.001 because such low values are not consistent with normal human physiology [19]. Barbanel et al. studied specific gravity and/or creatinine concentrations in 803,130 random urine specimens submitted to the laboratory. Out of these 13,467 specimens had both creatinine and specific gravity measurements performed and none of them met the lower limit of specific gravity (1.001) and creatinine (5 mg/dL). The patients who met one of the two criteria (creatinine <5.0 mg/dL or specific gravity <1.001) were neonatal or severely ill, unlike anyone in the workforce undergoing testing for abused drugs. Eleven patients met the criterion of substituted urine (creatinine < 5 mg/dL, specific gravity >1.020) but all of them were seriously or terminally ill [20].

Cook et al. evaluated freezing point depression osmolality for classifying random urine specimens defined as "substituted" under DOT (Department of Transportation) guidelines. Osmolality was measured in urine specimens (n = 66) with creatinine less than 5 mg/dL. The authors found that 62% of the specimens had specific gravity less than or equal to 1.001 and 52% had osmolality less than 50 mOsm/kg. Using a hydration experiment with 35 volunteers (volunteers drank at least 2,370 mL of fluid), the authors observed that the lowest achievable osmolality was 28 mOsm/kg. Polyuria disorder causes low urine osmolality and the lowest reported value is 18 mOsm/kg, although osmolality less than 23 mOsm/kg from water intoxication has resulted in death. The authors concluded that an osmolality cut-off for substituted urine can be set at <50 mOsm/kg [21].

Criteria for diluted urine as described by various investigators are summarized in Table 4.1.

Table 4.1 Criteria for diluted urine

Test	Values	Reference
Creatinine	<5 mg/dL[a]	SAMSHA guidelines
Specific gravity	1.0010 or above 1.020	SAMSHA guidelines
Creatinine	<45 mg/dL	
Specific gravity	1.007–1.035	12
Creatinine	<45 mg/dL	13
Creatinine	<20 mg/dL	Criteria used in many drug testing
Specific gravity	1.005–1.030	facilities including our facility
Creatinine	<10 mg/dL	11

[a]Inconsistent with normal human urine

6.4 Diluted Urine: Case Studies

The following cases were taken from MRO Case Studies, a publication of SAMHSA (Health and Human Services of the US Government) [22].

Case 1: The laboratory reported that the urine specimen submitted was substituted (creatinine concentration 1.5 mg/dL and specific gravity 1.0005). During the interview the donor claims to have been performing strenuous activity in a hot climate and drinking large amounts of fluid several days before drug testing. The MRO requested the agency to have the donor provide another urine specimen under similar condition using a direct observation collection process. The laboratory reports that the creatinine concentration in the urine specimen following supervised collection was 5.5 mg/dL and the specific gravity was 1.003. The MRO reported the result as "Refusal to Test (Substituted)."

Case 2: The laboratory reported that the creatinine concentration in the urine specimen was 1.0 mg/dL and specific gravity 1.0005. During the interview the donor had no explanation for such a diluted urine and the MRO reported the result to the agency as "Refusal to Test (Substituted)."

Case 3: The laboratory reported the test to be negative and dilute. The MRO is not required to interview the donor although the diluted specimen may be due to large amounts of fluid consumed by the person or use of diuretics. The Department of Transportation (DOT) requires an immediate collection of a second specimen using a direct observed collection procedure when the creatinine concentration for a negative-dilute specimen is between 2.0 and 5.0 mg/dL.

6.5 Do These Agents Work?

Flushing and detoxification are frequently advertised as effective means of passing drug tests. Many of the products on offer contain caffeine or other diuretics to increase the output of urine, sugar and natural or artificial flavoring agents. The objective is to produce dilute urine by the subject so that concentrations of abused drugs and or metabolites can be pushed below the recommended cut-off concentrations of the drugs of abuse testing program. Cone et al. evaluated the effect of excess fluid ingestion on false negative marijuana and cocaine urine test results. The authors studied the ability of Naturally Clean Herbal tea, Golden Seal root and hydrochlorothiazide to cause false negative results. Volunteers drank one gallon of water (divided into four doses over a 4-h period) or herbal tea or hydrochlorothiazide 22 h after smoking marijuana cigarettes or intranasal administration of cocaine. The creatinine levels dropped below the cut-off 2 h after intake of excessive fluid. Marijuana and cocaine metabolite levels (as measured by both EMIT and FPIA) decreased significantly and frequently switched from positive to negative in subjects after consuming two quarts of fluid. Even excess water was effective in diluting a urine specimen to cause false negative results. Consumption of herbal tea produced dilute urine faster compared to subjects who drank water alone [23].

Coleman and Baselt studied the efficacy of two products – Quick Flush (A–Z Enterprise, Sparks, NV) and Eliminator (New Vision Concepts, Phoenix, AZ) – to invalidate urine drug testing. Quick Flush involved the ingestion of 10 herbal tablets plus 80 drops of a liquid in 120 mL water every 10 min on three occasions as well as ingestion of an additional 240 mL of after each tablet-liquid repetition for a total amount of water of 1,980 mL. Eliminator involved ingestion of 480 mL of water beginning immediately after drug ingestion followed by ingestion of 60 g of a powder dissolved in 480 mL of water and then an additional 480 mL of water (1,440 mL water total) after 15 min. When volunteers ingested capsules containing various drugs/metabolites (amphetamine, benzoylecgonine, codeine and 9-carboxy

11-nor-delta-9-tetrahydrocannabinol; THC−COOH), and followed a treatment protocol involving one of these agents, significant reductions in drug or metabolite concentrations were observed for up to 24 h after ingestion as measured by the GC/MS analysis but the screening using RIA (radio immunoassay) was not affected much. In addition, water alone was approximately as effective as these commercials agents in reducing drug or metabolite levels in urine. The urinary pH, specific gravity or creatinine concentrations were within acceptable physiological limits. The authors concluded that an attempt to conceal drug abuse by water dilution is most likely to play a substantial role when concentrations of drugs are at or near the cut-off concentrations of immunoassays as with the terminal phase of drug elimination [24].

Diuretics are used in sports for two purposes; first to flush out previously taken banned substances by forced diuresis and second to achieve quick weight loss to qualify for a group within a lower weight class. The Medical Commission of the International Olympic Committee bans diuretics. There is no commercially available immunoassay for detecting diuretics such as hydrochlorothiazide in urine and a sophisticated technique such as liquid chromatography combined with tandem mass spectrometry is necessary to confirm the presence of diuretics in doping analysis [25]. Recently, a high throughput screening method for diuretics, masking agents along with central nervous system stimulants and opiates in urine specimens using ultra-performance liquid combined with tandem mass spectrometry (UPLC-MS/MS) has been described [26].

7 Herbals to Beat Drug Tests

Herbals are associated with workplace drug testing in two different ways:

1. There is a belief among drug abusers that certain herbals may help them to beat a workplace drug testing
2. When tested positive, some individuals deny any drug use and blame herbal remedies for their positive test results

There is a popular belief that drinking goldenseal tea may help a drug abuser to pass a drug test. In reality, drinking goldenseal tea produces a dark colored urine which can easily be identified visually. As discussed above, such a method is not effective to cheat on a drug test. Commonly used herbal products including ginkgo biloba, saw palmetto, St. John's wort, Siberian ginseng, garlic, green tea capsule, valerian and cranberry extract do not produce false positive test results in urine drug of abuse screening using EMIT assays [27]. Winek et al. analyzed 50 herbal supplements for potential interference with drugs of abuse screening of urine specimens using the fluorescence polarization immunoassays (FPIA, and ADX analyzer, Abbott Laboratories, Abbott Park IL) and found that none of the supplements in the concentration range screened showed any interference with FPIA assays as well as

Table 4.2 Common herbal supplements that do not interfere with workplace drug testing

Asian ginseng	Korean ginseng	Siberian ginseng
Brazilian tea	Peppermint tea	Green tea
Herbal laxative tea	Pleasant dream tea	Papaya herb tea
Licorice tea	Spearmint tea	Comfrey tea
Chamomile tea	Rose hip herb tea	Ginkgo biloba
Saw palmetto	Sage	Juniperus
St. John's wort	Garlic	Valerian
Cranberry extract	Strawberry	Red sorrel
Thymus	Lungwort leaves	Yellow dock root
Turkish bay leaves	Rosemary	Arnica
Queen of meadow	Senega	Caraway
Squaw vine	Barley grass	Purple sponge
Sunflower seeds	Eriodictyon	Humulus

analysis by thin layer chromatography [28]. Common herbal supplements that do not interfere with workplace drug testing are listed in Table 4.2.

Certain herbal supplements, especially supplements coming from overseas, may be contaminated with Western drugs. Floren and Fitter reported contamination of urine with diazepam and mefenamic acid from consumption of an Oriental remedy [29]. Liu et al. reported the presence of codeine in one antiasthmatic Oriental medicine [30]. Drinking coca tea may cause positive cocaine test results and there is an isolated report of a positive urinary cocaine test in a patient who was taking mugwort. Although cocaine is not present in mugwort, this patient was taking a contaminated product and tested positive for cocaine (see also Chap. 8).

8 Various Drugs and False Negative/Positive Screening Assay Results

Wagener et al. reported that ingestion of aspirin interfered with EMIT (Enzyme Multiplied Immunoassay Technique) drugs of abuse screening assays. The authors observed that urine specimens containing salicylate (15–420 mg/dL) may cause false negative test results using EMIT assays. Interestingly, when salicylate was added in vitro to urine specimens, no effect was observed, but when volunteers ingested aspirin tablets and their urine specimens were subsequently analyzed, negative bias was observed. The authors concluded that ingestion of therapeutic doses of aspirin may cause false negative results for drug screens of urine specimens by this method [31]. This is problematic because, if a urine specimen is tested negative by the immunoassay, GC/MS confirmation is not usually performed.

Another report in the literature indicated that ingestion of non-steroidal anti-inflammatory drugs ibuprofen or fenoprofen caused false positive results with the FPIA (Fluorescence polarization immunoassay on the TDx analyzer; Abbott Laboratories, Abbott Park, IL) benzodiazepine assays. The specimens containing fenoprofen tested positive by the FPIA assay for barbiturates. The authors concluded that both ibuprofen and fenoprofen caused false positive results with the FPIA assays for drugs of abuse screening [32]. Rollins et al. reported that there is a small likelihood of a false positive immunoassay screening results for marijuana metabolite (cannabinoids), benzodiazepines or barbiturates after acute or chronic ingestion of ibuprofen, or after chronic ingestion of fenoprofen or naproxen [33]. A false positive urine opiate screen associated with fluoroquinolone has also been reported [34]. Dextromethorphan is an antitussive agent which is found in many over the counter cough and cold medications. High dosage of dextromethorphan (over 30 mg) may produce positive false positive opiate and phencyclidine (PCP) test results with immunoassays. In addition, pheniramine and methylphenidate also produce false positive results with a PCP screen [35].

However, GC/MS confirmation step should be able to distinguish such false positive results from analytically true positive results.

9 Conclusions

A variety of products are available through the Internet and toll free telephone numbers purporting to enable users to pass drug testing by getting rid of unwanted drugs from the body prior to testing. In addition, the majority of manufacturers recommend drinking plenty of fluid along with these products in order to beat drug testing. Many of these products contain caffeine or diuretics and may produce diluted urine which should be easily identified by observing low creatinine concentration and specific gravity. It is important for the laboratory to document that information because diluted or substituted specimen can be considered as "refusal to test" and MRO can report that to the agency. In addition, contrary to myth, there is no herbal product on the market to the knowledge of this author that can successfully invalidate a workplace drug testing.

References

1. Mayrovitz HN, Sims N. Biophysical effects of water and synthetic urine on skin. Adv Skin Wound Care 2001; 14: 302–308.
2. Cook JD, Strauss KA, Caplan YH, Lodico CP et al. Urine pH: the effects of time and temperature after collection. J Anal Toxicol 2007; 31: 486–496.
3. Co-owners of the whizzinator pled guilty to conspiring to defeat federal drug test. United States Attorney's office: Western District of Pennsylvania. http://www.usdoj.gov/usao/paw/pr/2008_november_2008_11_24_03.html Accessed 4/14/2009.
4. Dasgupta A. The effect of adulterants and selected ingested compounds on drugs of abuse testing in urine. Am J Clin Pathol 2007; 228: 491–503.
5. Finkel KW. Water intoxication presenting as a suspected contaminated urine sample for drug testing. South Med J 2004; 97: 611–613.
6. Gardner JW, Gutmann FD. Fatal water intoxication of an army trainee during urine drug testing. Mil Med 2002; 167: 435–437.

7. Klonoff DC, Jurow AH. Acute water intoxication as a complication of urine drug testing in the workplace. JAMA 1991; 265: 84–85.
8. George S, Braithwaite. RA. An investigation into the extent of possible dilution of specimens received for urinary drugs of abuse screening. Addiction 1995; 90: 967–970.
9. Fraser AD, Zamecnik J, Keravel J, McGrath L, Wells J. Experience with urine drug testing by the correctional service of Canada. Forensic Sci Int 2001; 121: 16–22.
10. Jaffee WB, Trucco E, Teter C, Levy S et al. Focus on alcohol and drug abuse: ensuring validity in urine drug testing. Psychiatr Serv 2008; 59: 140–142.
11. Needleman SD, Porvaznik M. Creatinine analysis in single collection urine specimens. J Forensic Sci 1992; 37: 1125–1133.
12. Edwards C, Fyfe MJ, Liu RH, Walia AS. Evaluation of urine specimen adulteration indicators. J Anal Toxicol 1993; 17: 251–252 [Letter to the editor].
13. Luceri F, Godi F, Messeri G. Reducing false negative tests in urinary drugs of abuse screening. J Anal Toxicol 1997; 21: 244–245 [Letter to the editor].
14. Fraser AD, Zamecnik J. Impact of lowering the screening and confirmation cutoff values for urine drug testing based on dilution indicators. Ther Drug Monit 2003; 25: 723–727.
15. Soldin SJ, Morales AJ, D'Angelo LJ, Bogema SC, Hicks JC. The importance of lowering the cut-off concentrations of urine screening and confirmatory tests for benzoylecgonine/cocaine [Abstract]. Clin Chem 1991; 37: 993.
16. Luzzi VI, Saunders AN, Koenig JW, Turk J, Lo SF, Garg U, Dietzen DJ. Analytical performance of immunoassays for drugs of abuse below established cutoff values. Clin Chem 2004; 50: 717–722.
17. NLCP. State of Science-Update #1. Subject: Urine specimen validity testing: evaluation of scientific data used to define a urine specimen as substituted (February 14, 2000). http://workplace.samhsa.gov/ResourceCenter/resource.asp?RCategoryID=8$String+Regulations/Guidance
18. Cook JD, Caplan YH, LoDico CP, Bush DM. The characterization of human urine for specimen validity determination in workplace drug testing: a review. J Anal Toxicol 2000; 24: 579–588.
19. Edgell K, Caplan YH, Glass LR, Cook JD. The defined HHS/DOT substituted urine criteria validated through controlled hydration study. J Anal Toxicol 2002; 26: 419–423.
20. Barbanel CS, Winkelman JW, Fischer GA, King AJ. Confirmation of the department of transportation criteria for a substituted urine specimen. J Occup Environ Med 2002; 44: 407–416.
21. Cook JD, Hannon MW Sr, Vo T, Caplan YH. Evaluation of freezing point depression osmolality for classifying random urine specimens defined as substituted under HHS/DOT. J Anal Toxicol 2002; 26: 424–429.
22. MRO Case Studies (Health and Human Services of the US Government) 2005: (http://workplace.samhsa.gov/DrugTesting/Files_Drug_Testing/MROs/MRO%20Case%20Studies%20-%20February%202005.pdf)
23. Cone EJ, Lange R, Darwin WD. In vivo adulteration: excess fluid ingestion cause false negative marijuana and cocaine urine test results. J Anal Toxicol 1998; 22: 460–473.
24. Coleman DE, Baselt RC. Efficacy of two commercial products for altering urine drug test results. J Toxicol Clin Toxicol 1997; 35: 637–642.
25. Deventer K, Delbeke FT, Roels K, Van Ecnoo P. Screening for 18 diuretics and probenecid in doping analysis by liquid chromatography-tandem mass spectrometry. Biomed Chromatogr 2002; 16: 529–535.
26. Thorngren JO, Ostervall F, Garle M. A high performance throughput multicomponent screening method for diuretics, masked agents, central nervous system (CNS) stimulants and opiates in human urine by UPLC-Ms/Ms. J Mass Spectrom 2008; 43: 980–982.
27. Markowitz JS, Donovan JL, DeVance CL, Chavin KD. Common herbal supplements did not produce false positive results on urine drug screens analyzed by enzyme immunoassay. J Anal Toxcol 2004; 28: 272–273.

28. Winek CL, Elzein EO, Wahba WW, Feldman JA. Interference of herbal drinks with urinalysis for drugs of abuse. J Anal Toxicol 1993; 17: 246–247.
29. Floren AE, Fitter W. Contamination of urine with diazepam and mefenamic acid from an Oriental remedy. J Occup Med 1991; 33: 1168–1169.
30. Liu SY, Woo SO, Koh HL. HPLC and GC-MS screening of Chinese proprietary medicine for undeclared therapeutic substances. J Pharm Biomed Anal 2001; 24: 983–992.
31. Wagener RE, Linder MW, Valdes R Jr.. Decreased signal in Emit assays of drugs of abuse in urine after ingestion of aspirin: potential for false-negative results. Clin Chem 1994; 40: 608–612.
32. Larsen J, Fogerson R. Nonsteroidal anti-inflammatory drugs interfere in TDx assays for abused drugs. Clin Chem 1988; 34: 987–988.
33. Rollins DE, Jennison TA, Jones G. Investigation of interference of nonsteroidal anti-inflammatory drugs in urine tests for abused drugs. Clin Chem 1990; 36: 602–606.
34. Zacher JL, Givone DM. False-positive urine opiate screening associated with fluoroquinolone use. Ann Pharmacother 2004; 38: 1525–1528.
35. Marchei E, Pellegrini M, Pichini S, Martin I et al. Are false positive phencyclidine immunoassay instant-view multi test results caused by overdose concentrations of ibuprofen, metamizol and dextromethorphan?. Ther Drug Monit 2007; 29: 671–673.

Chapter 5
Household Chemicals and Internet Based Products for Beating Urine Drug Tests

Abstract People try to beat drug tests by adding various substances into urine specimens. Easily available household chemicals such as table salt, vinegar, lemon juice, bleach and liquid soap are a few examples of in vitro adulterants people use with a hope of beating drug tests. Most of these adulterants interfere with various immunoassays used for screening drugs/metabolites in urine specimens. However, all such chemicals except for Visine eye drops can be easily detected by performing specimen integrity testing (pH, creatinine, temperature and specific gravity) of the urine specimen. In the last 10–15 years many Internet based companies have been selling in vitro adulterants containing potassium nitrite, glutaraldehyde, pyridinium chlorochromate and Stealth (a combination of peroxidase and hydrogen peroxide). These chemicals are effective in modifying structures of certain drug/metabolites, especially marijuana metabolite, and may cause false negative test results in both immunoassay screening and gas chromatography/mass spectrometry (GC/MS) confirmation. Unfortunately, the presence of these compounds in urine specimens cannot be detected by routine specimen integrity testing. However, special dipstick tests and other tests are available in order to detect these adulterants in the urine.

Keywords Glutaraldehyde · Household chemicals · Internet based adulterants · Potassium nitrite

1 Introduction

People try to cheat drug testing by adding adulterants in vitro to urine after collection. These urinary adulterants can be either common household chemicals or chemicals sold by various Internet based companies claiming that such adulterants can invalidate any drug testing. Many household chemicals interfere with immunoassay screening of various drugs/metabolites if present in urine specimens. Moreover, certain chemicals sold though the Internet or by telephone contain very strong oxidizing agents and can invalidate both the screening assays and

A. Dasgupta, *Beating Drug Tests and Defending Positive Results*,
DOI 10.1007/978-1-60761-527-9_5, © Springer Science+Business Media, LLC 2010

the confirmation step by gas chromatography/mass spectrometry because these agents are capable of destroying drugs or drug metabolites in urine by oxidizing these molecules. Currently 90% of the estimated 55 million drug testings in the United States are performed on urine specimens that can be adulterated or diluted in order to cheat on drug testing. Presently, 15 states have enacted laws prohibiting the sale of urinary adulterants. A list of these states is given in Table 5.1.

Table 5.1 States that have taken legal steps against adulteration and drug fraud

State	Penalties
Arkansas	Class B misdemeanor
Illinois	Class four felony; minimum fine $1000
Kentucky	Class D felony; fine up to $10,000 and imprisonment up to 5 years
Louisiana	Fine up to $500, imprisonment up to 6 months or both
Maryland	Fine up to $1,000 or imprisonment up to 1 year for first violation. Stiffer penalty for subsequent offence
Nebraska	Class 1 misdemeanor; fine up to $1,000 or imprisonment up to 1 year or both
New Jersey	Imprisonment up to 18 months or fine up to $10,000 or both
North Carolina	Class 1 misdemeanor
Oklahoma	Misdemeanor; imprisonment up to 1 year or fine up to 10,000 or both
Oregon	Class B misdemeanor
Pennsylvania	Misdemeanor of third degree
South Carolina	Misdemeanor; first offence imprisonment up to 3 years or fine up to $5,000 or both. Stiffer penalty for subsequent violations
Texas	Class B misdemeanor; imprisonment up to 6 months or fine up to 4,000 or both
Virginia	Class 1 misdemeanor
Wyoming	Misdemeanor for first offence; imprisonment up to 6 months or fine up to $750 or both
	Felony for subsequent offence; imprisonment up to 5 years or fine up to 10,000 or both

2 Household Chemicals as Urinary Adulterants

Several household chemicals are used to invalidate drug of abuse testing in urine. The most commonly used chemicals are:

1. Sodium chloride
2. Household vinegar
3. Drano®, Joy®, hand soap
4. Liquid laundry bleach
5. Mary Jane's Super Cleaner 13

6. Ammonia
7. Sodium bicarbonate and sodium hypochlorite
8. Denture cleansing tablets (sodium perborate and salts)
9. Concentrated lemon juice
10. Ascorbic acid (Vitamin C)
11. Golden seal tea (produces dark urine)
12. Visine eye drops
13. Hydrogen peroxide
14. Ethanol and isopropanol

2.1 Effect of Various Adulterants on Immunoassay Screening

The immunoassay for 11-nor-9-carboxy-Δ^9-tetrahydrocannabinol, the major metabolite of marijuana (THC−COOH), is most susceptible to urine adulteration as many adulterants can cause false negative results if present in sufficient concentrations. Several studies have demonstrated that the pH of urine can have a significant effect on the results of drug screening tests. There are many readily available cleaning agents that, when added to urine in sufficient quantities, are capable of drastically altering the pH of urine [1–5].

Sodium chloride caused false negative results with several drugs tested by EMIT (Enzyme Multiplied Immunoassay Technique, Syva, San Jose, CA) and caused a slight decrease in measured concentrations of benzodiazepines by FPIA. However, sodium chloride has no effect on screening of amphetamines, barbiturates, benzodiazepines, phencyclidine, benzoylecgonine, opiates and cannabinoid (THC−COOH) using CEDIA assays (cloned enzyme donor immunoassay, Microgenics Corporation, Concord, CA). Sodium bicarbonate in sufficient amounts invalidates the EMIT opiate assay and the FPIA PCP assay, but does not interfere with CEDIA assays for screening drugs in urine specimens. Hydrogen peroxide caused false positive benzodiazepine results by FPIA [1,2]. In another report, the authors observed that a urine specimen tested negative for morphine, barbiturate and methadone using the EMIT assays, but showed the presence of all three drugs using thin layer chromatography. On further analysis of the specimen, it was found that the patient added sodium chloride to the specimen. When sodium chloride at different concentrations were added to urine specimens already supplemented with these drugs, the authors observed that at a sodium chloride concentration of 50 g/L, all specimens tested by EMIT assays switched from positive to negative, indicating that sodium chloride, if present in sufficient amounts, can invalidate these tests [3].

Uebel and Wium studied the effect of household chemicals sodium hypochlorite, Dettol (chloroxylenol, a topical over-the counter antiseptic popular in many countries outside US), glutaraldehyde, Pearl hand soap, ethanol, isopropanol and peroxide on cannabis and methaqualone tests using EMIT assays. Most of the agents tested interfered with the tests and the greatest effect was observed with glutaraldehyde and Pearl hand soap for methaqualone (false negative). Dettol and Pearl hand soap also caused false negative results in cannabis tests. Addition of isopropanol, ethanol and peroxide invalidated a methaqualone test [4].

Schwarzhoff and Cody studied the effect of 16 different adulterating agents: ammonia based cleaner, L-ascorbic acid (Vitamin C), Visine eye drops, Drano, golden seal root, lemon juice, lime solvent, Clorox, liquid hand soap, methanol, sodium chloride, tribasic potassium phosphate, toilet bowl cleaner (Vanish, Drackett Products), white vinegar, ionic detergent (Multi-Terge) and whole blood anticoagulated with EDTA on FPIA (fluorescence polarization immunoassay) assays for various abused drugs in urine specimens. The authors tested these adulterating agents at 10% by volume concentration of urine with the exception of Golden seal tea because of the insolubility. For Golden seal tea one capsule was suspended in 60 mL urine. Out of six drugs tested (benzoylecgonine, amphetamines, opiates, phencyclidine, THC metabolite and barbiturates), the cannabinoid test was most susceptible to adulteration. Approximately half of the agents tested (ascorbic acid, vinegar, bleach, lime solvent, Visine eye drops, and Golden seal) caused false negative. Both cannabinoid and opiate assays were susceptible to bleach and actual degradation of THC metabolite (11-nor-9-carboxy-Δ^9-tetrahydrocannabinol) was confirmed by GC/MS analysis. The PCP and benzoylecgonine analysis were affected by alkaline agents. The barbiturate assay was particularly sensitive to detergents and the only assay where authors observed false positive tests due to the presence of adulterants. Golden seal roots with its high content of insoluble plant material would be difficult to add to urine as an adulterant because it can be detected easily by visual observation. Nevertheless, Golden seal produces a significant effect on both THC metabolite and barbiturate assays at concentrations less than 1% due to probable binding of drugs to insoluble plant material [5]. Hydrogen peroxide results in false positive results with the FPIA assay for benzodiazepines. Some effects (false positive) may also be observed with the FPIA assay for marijuana metabolite.

Concentrated lemon juice usually has minimal effect on drugs of abuse testing by immunoassays. The presence of concentrated lemon juice can be easily detected in the urine specimen by the specimen integrity test because the pH is usually on the acidic side (pH 4 or less). Ascorbic acid can invalidate the assay of marijuana metabolite using the FPIA (false negative results). Interestingly, ascorbic acid causes false positive results with creatinine analysis using the assay kit available from the Abbott Laboratories. Uebel and Wium reported that addition of alcohol or isopropanol to urine specimen in any concentration (5, 10, 20 and 40%) invalidate the EMIT assay for methaqualone [4].

Baiker et al. reported that bleach containing hypochlorite not only affects immunoassay screening of cannabinoids but can also cause false negative results with the gas chromatography/mass spectrometric (GC/MS) confirmation step. Even a small amount of bleach (8–64 μL per milliliter of urine) can significantly affect determination of cannabinoids both by immunoassay screening (using a radioimmunoassay or the fluorescence polarization immunoassay by the Abbott Laboratories, Abbot Park, IL) as well as GC/Ms confirmation. The amount of decrease of signal is more dramatic with GC/MS confirmation [6]. Another report described adulteration of urine specimens with denture cleaning tablets containing 1.5% sodium perborate and various salts interfering with FPIA assays for 3,4-methylenedioxymethamphetamine (MDMA), benzoylecgonine and cannabinoids. The possible mechanism of interference is oxidation of drug/metabolite by sodium perborate. Moreover, salts also alter the ionic strength of urine and may interfere with the immunoassay employed (FPIA, Abbott Laboratories, Abbott Park, IL) [7].

The ability of Visine eye drops to cause false negative drug testing in the screening phase of the analysis is troublesome because the presence of components of Visine eye drops in adulterated urine cannot be detected by routine specimen integrity testing or any routine urine analysis. Pearson et al. studied in detail the effect of Visine eye drops on drugs of abuse testing as well as the mechanism by which components of Visine eye drops produces false negative drug testing results. Visine eye drops are effective in causing false negative results in the analysis of the THC metabolite 11-nor-9-carboxy-Δ^9-tetrahydrocannabinol. The gas chromatography/mass spectrometry analysis showed that there was no modification in the structure of THC metabolite by the components of Visine eye drops. At low concentrations of Visine, the false negative cannabinoid result was due to the benzalkonium chloride ingredient of Visine. Visine decreased the THC assay results in both EMIT –d.a.u. assays and Abuscreen (Abbott Laboratories), although Visine had no effect on glucose 6-phosphate dehydrogenase-drug conjugate used in the EMIT assay. Results of the ultrafiltration studies with Visine suggest that the THC metabolite partitions between the aqueous solvent and the hydrophobic interior of benzalkonium chloride micelles, thus reducing the availability of THC metabolite in the antibody based assay [8]. Visine eye drops and Ben Gay ointment can also cause false negative drug testing with sweat testing [9]. Components of Visine eye drops in urine may be detected by using high performance liquid chromatography combined with UV detection at 262 nm, a method originally developed for analysis of ophthalmic formulations [10].

2.2 *Effect of Various Household Adulterants on Specimen Integrity Testing*

As discussed in Chap. 4, both the collection site and the laboratory have a number of mechanisms to detect potentially invalid specimens. The temperature of urine, for instance, should be within 32–38 °C (89.6–100.4 °F). The temperature of urine should be checked within 4 min of collection although urine specimens may retain temperature for 15 min and may be warmer than 33 °C. The specific gravity should be between 1.005 and 1.030 and the pH should be between 4.5 and 8.0. The creatinine concentration should be 20–400 mg/dL. A specimen is considered as diluted if the creatinine is <20 mg/dL and the specific gravity is less than 1.003. The laboratory should perform creatinine and pH analysis of all specimens submitted for drugs of abuse testing. Additional tests are also recommended to detect the presence of other adulterants. Determination of specific gravity is mandatory for any specimen with a creatinine concentration of less than 20 mg/dL. Substituted urine specimens have creatinine concentrations <5 mg/dL and a specific gravity 1.001 or over 1.020. The urine is adulterated if the pH is <3 or >11.

Adulteration with sodium chloride at a concentration necessary to produce a false negative result always produces a specific gravity over 1.035 (Table 5.2). Use of household chemicals such as bleach, acid, soap, and detergent, as well as adulteration with vinegar, may alter the pH of urine to a value outside the physiological range and maybe detected by specimen integrity tests. For example, ascorbic acid at a 10% concentration produces a pH of 3.0 which is outside the acceptable range and 10% Drano produces a pH of 12.0, but 10% bleach produces a pH of 6.7 which is within the acceptable limit [5]. The presence of ammonia in the specimen can be easily identified by the characteristic odor and the pH would also be outside the acceptable range. Contrary to popular belief, Mary Jane's Super Cleaner 13 can be detected by specimen integrity testing and is not so effective to cheat a drug test. Specimens adulterated with liquid soap are usually cloudy (Table 5.2). Unfortunately, Visine eye drops do not change any parameter of specimen integrity testing and their presence in the urine specimen cannot be detected by such tests. Effects of these adulterants on urine specimen integrity testings are given in Table 5.2.

Table 5.2 Adulterants and specimen integrity testing

	Specimen integrity tests[a]			
Household chemicals	pH	Creatinine	Temperature	Specific gravity
Diluted urine		X	X	X
Sodium chloride				X
Vinegar	X			
Laundry bleach	X			
Liquid soap	X			Cloudy
Drano®	X			
Sodium bicarbonate	X			
Sodium hypochlorite	X			
Mary Jane's Super Cleaner 13	X			
Lemon juice	X			
Golden Seal				Dark urine
Ascorbic acid (Vitamin C)	X			
Visine eye drops[a]				
Glutaraldehyde[a]				
Potassium nitrite (Urine Luck)[a]				
Pyridinium chlorochromate[a]				
Papain[a]				
Stealth[a]				

X: Abnormal test indicative of the adulterant

[a]Cannot be detected by routine urine specimen integrity testing

3 Internet Based Urinary Adulterants

Many Internet based companies sell adulterants which should be added in vitro to the urine specimen after collection in order to invalidate drug testing. Fortunately, due to strict state laws, these adulterants cannot be shipped into certain states but unfortunately these companies still exist because not all states have such laws and Federal laws are not well defined at this point. Although sold by many companies, the basic products are strong oxidizing agents including potassium nitrite, pyridinium chlorochromate, Stealth (a combination of peroxidase and hydrogen peroxide) and glutaraldehyde. The presence of any of these compounds in the urine specimen cannot be detected by routine specimen integrity testing. Therefore, drug testing facilities have to adapt to new testings in order to detect these adulterants if present in submitted specimens. Fortunately, spot tests and readily available dipstick tests as well as tests that can be automated are available to deal with this problem. If any such adulterant can be detected in a specimen, it should be considered as "refusal to testing" and appropriate disciplinary action can be taken against such persons who attempt to beat drug tests. In certain states, attempt to beat a drug test or possession of an adulterant is against the law and such individuals can be prosecuted.

3.1 Adulteration Product Urine Luck

Wu et al. reported that the active ingredient of "Urine Luck" is 200 mmol/L of pyridinium chlorochromate (PCC). The package insert of Urine Luck recommends dilution of 90–150 mL of urine (3–5 oz) with the vial containing 7 mL of the adulterant, producing a final PCC concentration of 47–78 mg/mL. The authors reported a decrease in the response rate for all EMIT II drug screens and for the Abuscreen (Roche Diagnostics, Indianapolis, IN) morphine and THC assays at a PCC concentration of 100 mg/mL. In contrast, Abuscreen amphetamine assays produced a higher response rate for amphetamine and no effect was observed on the results of benzoylecgonine, and PCP. This adulteration of urine did not alter GC/MS confirmation of methamphetamine, benzoylecgonine and PCP or their deuterated internal standard, but decreased GC/MS recovery of opiates at both intermediate (50 mg/mL of PCC) and high (100 mg/mL of PCC) was observed. In addition, apparent concentrations of marijuana and its deuterated metabolite were also reduced with all concentrations of PCC tested. The authors also observed that two urine specimens out of 50 submitted to the authors' laboratory under chain of custody for drugs of abuse analysis tested positive for PCC [11]. Paul et al. also studied the effect of "Urine Luck" on testing for drugs of abuse. When THC−COOH (the metabolite of marijuana which is usually determined in urine) containing urine specimens were treated with 2 mmol/L of PCC, 58–100% of the THC−COOH was lost. The loss increased with decreasing pH and increasing time of incubation (0–3 days). There was no effect on the concentration of free codeine or free morphine if the pH of the urine was in the range of 5–7, but at lower pH significant loss of free morphine was observed and the loss of free morphine varied from 1 to 100%. Amphetamine, methamphetamine, benzoylecgonine, and PCP remained unaffected by PCC at urine pH 3–7 for 3 days [12].

3.2 Adulteration Products Containing Nitrite

The urine adulteration products "Klear" and "Whizzies" contain potassium nitrite. The product "Klear" comes in two microtubes containing 500 mg of white crystalline material. This compound readily dissolves in urine without affecting colour, pH or temperature. Klear may cause a false negative GC/MS confirmation for marijuana metabolite (THC–COOH). ElSohly et al. first reported this product as potassium nitrite and provided evidence that nitrite leads to decomposition of ions of THC–COOH and its internal standard. The authors reported that using a bisulfite step at the beginning of sample preparation could eliminate such interference because sodium bisulfite in sufficient amounts (250 mg of solid sodium bisulfite or 1 mL of 25% sodium bisulfite added to the urine specimen) can destroy all nitrite present in the sample. In addition, the authors warned against acidification of urine prior to adding sodium bisulfite because degradation of THC–COOH takes place during acidification [13].

Tsai et al. further investigated the effect of nitrite on immunoassay screening of other drugs. These drugs included cocaine metabolites, morphine, THC metabolites (THC–COOH), amphetamine, and phencyclidine. Nitrite at a concentration of 1.0 M had no effect on the Abuscreen ONLINE assay (Roche Diagnostics). At a higher nitrite concentration, the amphetamine assay becomes more sensitive (detects more drug than expected), and the THC metabolite assay becomes less sensitive (detects less drug than expected). Interestingly, no effect of nitrite was seen on two on-site drug testing assays; Abuscreen ONTRAK assays and ONTRAK TESTCUP-5 assays. The GC/MS analyses of benzoylecgonine, morphine, amphetamine, and phencyclidine were not affected by nitrite adulteration while recovery of the THC metabolite along with the internal standard was significantly reduced. Again, this interference could be eliminated by bisulfite treatment. The presence of nitrite in the urine specimen arising from microorganism, pathological condition or medication did not interfere with the GC/MS confirmation of THC–COOH [14]. Both duration of nitrite exposure and the urine matrix also affect the THC–COOH assay. In an in vitro study, 40 clinical urine specimens confirmed positive for THC–COOH were supplemented with 1.15 or 0.30 M nitrite. The results indicated that the pH of the urine, and the original drug concentrations, play major roles in dictating the effectiveness of nitrite in causing false negative THC metabolite tests. With acidic pH, significant decreases in the immunoassay screening results can be observed in all urine specimens within 4 h of adulteration and nitrite regardless of original concentrations of THC–COOH (range of concentrations 33–488 ng/mL as determined by GC/MS), specimens tested negative by immunoassays after 1 day. In contrast, the immunoassay results of urine specimens with basic or neutral pH were less affected by nitrite exposure. Approximately two thirds of the samples with pH values greater than 7.0 were immunoassay positive even 3 days after supplementing with nitrite [15].

Nitrite in urine may arise in vivo and is found in urine in low concentration. Patients receiving medications such as nitroglycerin, isosorbide dinitrate, nitroprusside and ranitidine may have increased nitrite levels in their blood. However, concentrations of nitrite were below 36 μg/mL in specimens cultured positive for microorganisms, and nitrite concentrations were below 6 μg/mL in patients receiving medications that are known to metabolize to nitrite. Nitrite and nitrate salts in very small quantities are used as a food preservative for meats to delay decomposition and maintain color for consumer appeal. The concentration of nitrite is very low at 50–200 parts per million. Some vegetables such as spinach, lettuce, celery and potato are also rich in nitrite. However, consumption of vegetables and nitrite preserved meat results in to an estimated 0.8–8.4 mg of nitrite per day. Most of this nitrite is decomposed by gastric juice and by oxygenated hemoglobin in the red blood cell. Therefore, under such circumstances, the urinary nitrite concentration should not exceed 1 μg/mL. On the other hand, nitrite concentrations were 1,910–12,200 μg/mL in urine specimens adulterated with nitrite [16].

3.3 Adulteration with Glutaraldehyde Containing Products

Glutaraldehyde has also been used as an adulterant to mask urine drug tests [17]. This product is available under the trade name of "UrinAid." The manufacturer, Byrd Laboratories (Topanga, CA), sells this product for $20–30 per kit. Each kit contains 4–5 mL glutaraldehyde solution, which is added to 50–60 mL of urine. Glutaraldehyde solutions are available in hospitals and clinics as a cleaning or sterilizing agent. A 10% solution of glutaraldehyde is available from pharmacies as over the counter medication for treatment of warts. Glutaraldehyde at a concentration of as low as 0.75% volume can lead to false negative screening results for a cannabinoid test using the EMIT II drugs of abuse screen (Syva, Palo Alto, CA). Amphetamine, methadone, benzodiazepine, opiate and cocaine metabolite tests can also produce false negative results at glutaraldehyde concentrations of 1−2% using EMIT immunoassays. At a concentration of 2% by volume, the assay of cocaine metabolite is significantly affected (apparent loss of 90% sensitivity). A loss of 80% sensitivity was also observed with the benzodiazepine assay.

Wu et al. reported that glutaraldehyde also interfered with the Microgenics CEDIA (cloned enzyme donor immunoassay) assays for screening of amphetamines, barbiturates, benzodiazepines, cocaine, opiates, phencyclidine and marijuana assays. CEDIA produced strong interferences for most drugs in the presence of glutaraldehyde, detergent and high concentrations of bleach and Drano. Minimal or selective interference was observed with golden seal tea, lemon juice, Visine and low concentrations of bleach and Drano. Essentially no interference was observed with sodium chloride, bicarbonate or vinegar [18]. Goldberger and Caplan reported that glutaraldehyde caused false negative results with EMIT but also caused false positive phencyclidine results with the FPIA (Abbott Laboratories) and Kinetic Interaction of Microparticles in a Solution Immunoassay (KIMS, Roche Diagnostics) [19].

3.4 Stealth as a Urinary Adulterant

Stealth is an adulterant advertised as an effective way to escape detection in a urine drug test. Stealth consists of two vials, one containing a powder (peroxidase) and another containing a liquid (hydrogen peroxide). Both products are added to the urine specimen. The presence of Stealth in a urine specimen cannot be detected by routine determination of parameters such as creatinine, pH, specific gravity, color, chloride, urea, blood glucose or nitrite. Stealth is capable of producing false negative results using both Roche ONLINE and Microgenics CEDIA immunoassay methods if marijuana metabolites, LSD (lysergic acid diethylamide) or opiates (morphine) are present in the urine at 125–150% of cut-off values. Adulteration of an authentic positive sample provided by a marijuana user caused that sample to screen negative using these immunoassay reagents [20]. Low concentration of morphine (2,500 ng/mL) could be effectively masked by Stealth, but higher concentrations (6,000 ng/mL) tested positive by immunoassay (Roche ONLINE and Microgenics CEDIA immunoassay). GC/MS confirmation can also be affected if Stealth is present in the urine. Cody et al. reported that GC/MS analysis of Stealth adulterated urine using standard procedures proved unsuccessful in several cases, and in 4 out of 12 cases neither the drug nor the internal standard was recovered. However, addition of sodium disulfite to the aliquots prior to extraction sometimes allowed recovery of both drug and the internal standard, but in some specimens 17% reduction in morphine and 30% reduction in codeine concentration were observed. In other cases, there was essentially no difference in concentration observed before or after adulteration, with or without disulfite treatment. The authors concluded that, unless the opiate concentration is near cut-off, the specimen is likely to be positive during immunoassay screening. Therefore, disulfite treatment should be considered if a specimen tests positive by the immunoassay but the opiate and the respective internal standard cannot be recovered during GC/MS confirmation [21].

Paul and Jacobs studied the effect of oxidizing adulterants on urine specimens containing 40 ng/mL of THC–COOH. The authors used horseradish peroxidase with an activity of 10 units/mL, and extracts from 2.5 g of red radish, Japanese radish, horseradish, and black mustard seeds all with 10 mmol/L of hydrogen peroxide as oxidizing adulterants and observed that all these oxidizing agents destroyed most the THC–COOH (>95%) within 48 h of exposure. In addition, other oxidizing agents such as chromate, nitrite, permanganate, and hydrogen peroxide in ferrous ammonium sulfate (Fenton's reagent) also destroyed most of THC–COOH present in urine specimens. Some losses were also observed with persulfate and periodate (25%) [22].

3.5 Papain as Urinary Adulterant

Papain is a cysteine with intrinsic ester hydrolysis capability. The presence of papain in urine cannot be detected by routine specimen integrity testing. Although papain has virtually no effect on determination of amphetamines, barbiturates, cocaine, opiate and phencyclidine, there was an average of 50% decline in THC−COOH concentration after 72 h in the urine specimen containing 10 mg/mL of papain (pH of urine: 6.2). GC/MS analysis of THC−COOH and HPLC-UV (high performance liquid chromatography combined with ultra-violet detection) analysis of nor-diazepam showed 66% and 24% reduction in concentrations respectively [23].

4 Detection of Internet Based Adulterants

As mentioned before, routine specimen integrity tests are ineffective to detect the presence of any of these adulterants in urine specimens. Therefore, laboratories need to apply special testing procedures to detect such adulterants. Such a process is crucial for promoting drug free workplace culture. In addition, SAMHSA also requires that such tests should be performed to identify these adulterants if present in urine specimens submitted for workplace drug testing. Adulteration of a specimen may also be considered as "refusal to testing" by the medical review officer (MRO), and an individual may be denied employment. The MRO may also request another collection of a specimen using direct observation. Under any circumstances it is vital for a laboratory to identify an adulterated specimen.

4.1 Testing for Urine Luck

Various spot tests are available for detecting the presence of urine luck (PCC) if present in the urine specimen. Wu et al. also described the protocol for detection of PCC in urine using spot tests. The indicator solution contains 10 g/L of 1,5-diphenylcarbazide in methanol. The indicator detects the presence of chromium ion and is colorless when prepared. Two drops of indicator solution is added to 1.0 mL of urine. If a reddish-purple color develops, the test is positive. A strong absorption peak can be observed at 550 nm which is characteristic of this spot test because neither the colorless indicator solution not PCC adulterated urine absorb at 550 nm [11]. Paul et al. used 1,5-diphenylcarbazide (DPC) for detection of PCC in urine. When this reagent was added, a red-violet color appeared immediately if PCC was present. The chromium-DPC complex showed a characteristic absorption peak at 544 nm and a shoulder peak at 575 nm. The ratio of absorption can be used to detect the presence of PCC as chromium in urine, and concentration of chromium can be estimated by measuring absorption at 544 nm, with a linear association between concentrations of 0.5–20 μg/mL [12]. Addition of a few drops of PCC adulterated urine to approximately 0.5 mL/L of potassium iodide solution followed by addition of a few drops of 2N hydrochloric acid leads to liberation of iodine from potassium iodide, and this can also be used as a spot test to detect PCC. Addition of four to five drops of 3% hydrogen peroxide in approximately 200 μL of urine adulterated with PCC (approximately six to seven drops from a transfer pipette) caused rapid formation of a dark brown color (due to reduction of heptavalent chromium by hydrogen peroxide) and a dark brown precipitate appeared on standing. In contrast, unadulterated urine turned colorless after addition of hydrogen peroxide [24].

Freslew et al. described a capillary ion electrophoresis technique for detecting chromate ion, as well as nitrite ion, in urine specimens suspected of adulteration [25]. The 1,5-diphenylcarbazide colorimetric test for chromate, which can be easily automated, can serve as a screening test. Capillary electrophoretic analysis can be used to confirm the presence of chromate in adulterated specimen, if necessary. A good correlation was observed between chromate concentrations in urine using the colorimetric test and capillary electrophoretic analysis [26]. Paul described six spectroscopic methods for detection of oxidants including chromate. The presence of oxidants (as adulterants in urine) was established by initial oxidation of ferrous to ferric ion and then detecting ferric ion by chromogenic oxidation or complex formation. The author used *N,N*-dimethylamino-1,4-phenylenediamine, 2, 2′-azino-bis (3-ethylbenzthiazoline-6-sulfonic acid or 2-amino-para-cresol for chromogenic oxidation. The reagents for the chromogenic complex formation were xylenol orange, 8-hydroxy-7-iodo-5-quinolinesulfonic acid and 4,5-dihydroxy-1,3-benzene-disulfonic acid [27].

4.2 Testing for Nitrite

The presence of high amounts of nitrite as expected in adulterated urine can be easily identified by simple spot test. Addition of a few drops of a nitrite adulterated urine specimen to 0.5 mL of 1% potassium permanganate solution followed by addition of a few drops of 2N hydrochloric acid turns a pink permanganate solution colorless with effervescence. The presence of very high glucose in urine (glucose > 1,000 mg/dL) and ketone bodies may cause a false positive. However, it takes approximately 2–3 min for the solution to turn colorless. On the other hand, if nitrite is present the solution turns colorless immediately. Another spot test to detect nitrite uses 1% potassium iodide solution. Addition of a few drops of nitrite adulterated urine to 0.5 mL of potassium iodide solution followed by addition of a few drops of 2N hydrochloric acid results in immediate release of iodine from the colorless potassium iodide solution. When this solution is shaken with *n*-butanol, the iodine is transferred to the organic phase showing its characteristic color. If no nitrite is present, the potassium iodide solution remains colorless. There is no interference from high glucose or ketone bodies if present in the urine [24].

Nitrite can be detected by diazotizing sulfanilamide and coupling the product with *N*-(1-naphthyl)ethylenediamine. The presence of nitrite in urine can also be confirmed by analysis using high performance liquid chromatography using a Dionex IonPac AS 14 analytical column with an anion self-generating suppressor and conductivity detector. The authors used potassium bromide as the internal standard. The mobile phase composition was 3.5 mM sodium carbonate and 1 mM sodium bicarbonate. The separation was achieved under isocratic condition. Using a single point calibration, the assay was linear up to a nitrite concentration of 12,000 μg/mL. The detection limit was 30 μg/mL [28]. Kinkennon et al. described a capillary electrophoresis method for detection of nitrite in urine specimens suspected of adulteration. The method involved separation of nitrite by capillary electrophoresis and direct UV detection at 214 nm. Separation was achieved by using a bare fused silica capillary column and a 25 mM phosphate buffer at pH 7.5. The method was linear for a nitrite concentration of 80–1500 μg/mL, with a limit of detection of 20 μg/mL. However, CrO_4^{2-} and $S_2O_8^{2-}$, as well as high concentrations of Cl^-, interfered with the chromatography [29].

4.3 Testing for Stealth

Valtier and Cody described a rapid color test to detect the presence of Stealth in urine. Addition of 10 μL of urine to 50 μL of TMB (tetramethylbenzidine) working solution followed by addition of 500 μL of 0.1 M phosphate buffer solution caused a dramatic color change of the specimen to dark brown. Peroxidase activity could also be monitored by using a spectrophotometer. Routine specimen integrity check using pH, creatinine, specific gravity and temperature did not detect the presence of Stealth in urine [30]. Our experience shows that if a few drops of a urine specimen adulterated with Stealth is added to potassium dichromate followed by few drops of 2N hydrochloric acid, a deep blue color develops immediately, which usually fades with time.

4.4 Testing for Glutaraldehyde

Although the presence of glutaraldehyde as an adulterant in urine can be detected by gas chromatography/mass spectrometry, Wu et al. described a simple fluorometric method for the detection of glutaraldehyde in urine. When 0.5 mL of urine was heated with 1.0 mL of 7.7 mmol/L potassium dihydrogen phosphate (pH 3.0) saturated with diethylthiobarbituric acid for 1 h at 96–98 °C in a heating block, a yellow green fluorophore developed if glutaraldehyde was present. Shaking the specimen with *n*-butanol resulted in the transfer of this adduct to the organic layer which can be viewed under long wavelength UV light. Glutaraldehyde in urine can also be estimated using a fluorometer [31].

4.5 Onsite Adulteration Check and Automated Assays

Standard urinalysis test strips such as Multistix from Bayer Diagnostics and Combur-Test from Roche Diagnostics are sometimes used to detect the presence of adulterants in urine. However, among various pads in the test strip, only pads for detection of nitrite and pH have some value. The specific gravity test does not differentiate between specific gravity of 1.000 and 1.005, and therefore it is very difficult to apply it to identify substituted or diluted urine. The nitrite pad also detects a clinically significant range. A glucose pad can also show strong positive reaction in the presence of various oxidants if present in the urine.

More recently, on-site adulterant detection devices have become commercially available. These dipstick devices offer an advantage over spot tests because an adulteration check can also be performed at the collection site. King evaluated performance of AdultaCheck 4 test strips for detection of adulterants at the point of collection of urine specimen and observed that AdultaCheck 4 is a cost-effective efficient dipstick test to detect adulterants in urine. Creatinine pad determines whether the urine is diluted, the nitrite pad detects nitrite containing adulterants such as Klear and Whizzies, and the glutaraldehyde pad detects glutaraldehyde containing adulterants such as Urine Luck, Amber -13, and THC Free. The pH pad can detect the presence of basic adulterants such as bleach or Drano which push urine pH over 10 [32]. Peace and Tarnai evaluated the performance of three on-site devices, Intect 7 (Branan Medical Corporation), MASK Ultrascreen (Kacey Inc) and AdultaCheck 4 (Sciteck Diagnostics). Intect 7 can simultaneously test for creatinine, nitrite, glutaraldehyde, pH, specific gravity, pyridinium chlorochromate (PCC) and bleach. Ultrascreen tests for creatinine, nitrite, pH, specific gravity and oxidants. AdultaCheck 4 tests creatinine, nitrite, glutaraldehyde and pH. The authors adulterated urine specimens with Stealth, Urine Luck, Instant Clean ADD-IT-ive and Klear at their optimum usage concentrations and concluded that Intect 7 was most sensitive and correctly identified adulterants. AdultaCheck 4 did not detect Stealth, Urine Luck or Instant Clean ADD-it-ive. Ultra Screen detected a broader range of adulterants than AdultaCheck 4. However, in practice it only detected these adulterants at levels well above their optimum usage, making it less effective than Intect 7 [33]. However, King reported that AdultaCheck 4 is an excellent way to detect contamination in urine specimens [34]. AdultaCheck 6 or Intect 7 test strips can determine a range of creatinine values, although the precise concentration of creatinine cannot be determined. Similarly, neither test strip can determine precisely the pH of a urine specimen but can only show the range. However, AdultaCheck 6 and Intect 7 test strips are capable of successfully identifying urine specimens with abnormally low creatinine concentrations and/or pH [35]. Now AdultaCheck 10 is also available from Sciteck (Asheville, NC) which tests for specific gravity, pH abnormal (range 2–12), pH normal (range 5–9), oxidant, creatinine, nitrite, aldehyde, chromate, peroxidase and halogen/bleach.

In addition, liquid reagents are also available which can be adopted in open channels of various automated chemistry analyzers used in clinical laboratories. Liquid reagents are available from Chimera Research and Chemical Company (now Sciteck, Asheville, NC) for detecting nitrite, pH, aldehyde, halogens, chromate, oxidants, creatinine and pH.

5 Federal Guidelines for Additional Testing to Detect Adulterants

SAMSHA guidelines requires additional tests for urine specimens with abnormal physical characteristics or ones that show characteristics of an adulterated specimen during initial screening or confirmatory tests (non-recovery of internal standard, unusual response, etc.). A pH less than 3 or more than 11, and nitrite concentrations greater than 500 μg/mL, indicate the presence of adulterants. A nitrite colorimetric test or a general oxidant colorimetric test can be performed to identify nitrite. Both chromium(III) and chromium(VI) are used for chrome plating, dyes and pigments, leather tanning, and wood preserving. In addition, chromium(III) is an essential nutrient and is always present in humans. However, chromium(VI) is toxic and is used as a urinary adulterant to beat drug test. The presence of chromium(VI) in a urine specimen is indicative of adulteration at a cut-off concentration of 50 μg/mL. The presence of chromium in a urine specimen can be confirmed by a chromium colorimetric test or a general test for the presence of oxidant. A confirmatory test can be performed using multi-wavelength spectrophotometry, ion chromatography, atomic absorption spectrophotometry, capillary electrophoresis or inductively coupled plasma mass spectrometry. The halogens fluorine, chlorine, bromine and iodine are found in nature and these halide salts are also found in urine, for example sodium chloride. However, elemental halogen (for example, pure bromine or iodine) can be used as adulterants. The presence of these elemental halogens should be confirmed by a halogen colorimetric test or a general test for the presence of oxidants. Confirmatory tests may employ multi-wavelength spectrophotometry, ion chromatography, atomic absorption spectrophotometry, capillary electrophoresis or inductively couples plasma mass spectrometry. The presence of glutaraldehyde should be detected by a general aldehyde test or the characteristic immunoassay response in one or more drug immunoassay tests for initial screening. The presence of pyridinium chlorochromate should be confirmed by using a general test for the presence of oxidant and a GC/MS confirmatory test. The presence of a surfactant should be verified by using a surfactant colorimetric test with a greater than or equal to 100 μg/mL dodecylbenzene sulfonate equivalent cut-off. Jones et al. described a modified methylene blue procedure for detection and quantitation of surfactants in urine. Based on the analysis of negative samples, an anionic surfactant level of 100 μg/mL or greater could be considered adulterated, but most likely such specimens will have levels greater than 800 μg/mL [36].

6 A Case Study

A laboratory reported that a urine specimen submitted for testing was adulterated and the concentration of nitrite was 850 μg/mL which was significantly above the cut-off 500 μg/mL. During the interview with the MRO, the donor claimed to eat cured meat for dinner but eating nitrite containing food could not elevate nitrite concentration of urine over 500 μg/mL. Because the donor did not have a legitimate explanation for high nitrite in the urine specimen, the MRO reported the test as "Refusal to Test" (adulterated nitrite 850 μg/mL) [37].

7 Conclusions

Both household chemicals and Internet based chemicals are used by individuals to cheat workplace drug testing. Although the presence of many household adulterants except for Visine eye drops can be easily detected in the adulterated urine, Internet based adulterants containing nitrite, pyridinium chlorochromate, glutaraldehyde, peroxidase/peroxide and papain cannot be detected by checking pH, temperature, specific gravity, and creatinine concentration of the urine specimens. Fortunately, various tests are available to detect such adulterants and drug testing facilities must have protocols to test for such adulterants because these adulterants are capable of causing false negative test results in both screening and confirmation step using GC/MS, especially for the presence of marijuana tested as marijuana metabolite (THC−COOH).

References

1. Warner A. Interference of household chemicals in immunoassay methods for drugs of abuse. Clin Chem 1989; 35: 648–651.
2. Wu AH, Forte E, Casella G, Sun K et al. CEDIA for screening drugs of abuse in urine and effect of adulterants. J Forensic Sci 1995; 40: 614–618.
3. Kim HU, Cerceo E. Interference by NaCl with the EMIT method of analysis for drugs of abuse. Clim Chem 1976; 22: 1936 [Letter to the Editor].
4. Uebel RA, Wium CA. Toxicological screening for drugs of abuse in samples adulterated with household chemicals. S Afr Med J 2002; 92: 547–549.
5. Schwarzhoff R, Cody JT. The effects of adulterating agents on FPIA analysis of urine for drugs of abuse. J Anal Toxicol 1993; 17: 14–17.
6. Baiker C, Serrano L, Lindner B. Hypochlorite adulteration of urine causing decreased concentration of delta-9-THC−COOH by GC/MS. J Anal Toxicol 1994; 18: 101–103.
7. Stolk LM, Scheijen JL. Urine adulteration with denture cleaning tablets [letter]. J Anal Toxicol 1997; 21: 403.
8. Pearson SD, Ash KO, Urry FM. Mechanism of false negative urine cannabinoid immunoassay screens by Visine eye drops. Clin Chem 1989; 35: 636–638.
9. Fogerson R, Schoendorfer D, Fay J, Spiehler V. Qualitative detection of opiates in sweat by EIAS and GC–MS. J Anal Toxicol 1997; 21: 451–458.
10. Rojsitthisak P, Wichitnithad W, Pipitharome O, Sanphanya K, Thanawattanawanich P. Simple HPLC determination of benzalkonium chloride in ophthalmic formulations containing antazoline and tetrahydrozoline. PDA J Pharm Sci Technol 2005; 59: 323–327.
11. Wu A, Bristol B, Sexton K, Cassella-McLane G, Holtman V, Hill DW. Adulteration of urine by urine luck. Clin Chem 1999; 45: 1051–1057.
12. Paul BD, Martin KK, Maguilo J, Smith ML. Effects of pyridinium chlorochromate adulterant (Urine Luck) on testing of drugs of abuse and a method for quantitative detection of chromium(VI) in urine. J Anal Toxicol 2000; 24: 233–237.

13. ElSohly MA, Feng S, Kopycki WJ, Murphy TP, Jones AB, Davis A, Carr D. A procedure to overcome interferences caused by adulterant "Klear" in the GC-MS analysis of 11-nor-Δ9-THC-9-COOH. J Anal Toxicol 1997; 20: 240–242 [Letter to the editor].
14. Tsai SC, ElSohly MA, Dubrovsky T, Twarowska B, Towt J, Salamone SJ. Determination of five abused drugs in nitrite-adulterated urine by immunoassay and gas chromatography-mass spectrometry. J Anal Toxicol 1998; 22: 474–480.
15. Tsai LS, ElSohly MA, Tsai SF, Murphy TO, Twarowska B, Salamone SJ. Investigation of nitrite adulteration on the immunoassay and GC-MS analysis of cannabinoids in urine specimens. J Anal Toxicol 2000; 24: 708–714.
16. Urry. F, Komaromy-Hiller G, Staley B, Crockett D, Kushnir M, Nelson G, Struempler R. Nitrite adulteration of workplace drug testing specimens: sources and associated concentrations of nitrite and distinction between natural sources and adulteration. J Anal Toxicol 1998; 22: 89–95.
17. George S, Braithwaite RA. The effect of glutaraldehyde adulteration of urine specimens on Syva EMIT II drugs of abuse assay. J Anal Toxicol 1996; 20: 195–196.
18. Wu AH, Forte E, Casella G, Sun K, Hemphill G, Forey R, Schanzenback H. CEDIA for screening drugs of abuse in urine and the effect of adulterants. J Forensci Sci 1995; 40: 614–618.
19. Goldberger BA, Caplan YH. Effect of glutaraldehyde (UrinAid) on detection of abused drugs in urine by immunoassay [Letter]. Clin Chem 1994; 40: 1605–1616.
20. Cody JT, Valtier S. Effects of Stealth adulteration on immunoassay testing for drugs of abuse. J Anal Toxicol 2001; 25: 466–470.
21. Cody JT, Valtier S, Kuhlman J. Analysis of morphine and codeine in samples adulterated with Stealth. J Anal Toxicol 2001; 25: 572–575.
22. Paul BD, Jacobs A. Effects of oxidizing adulterants on detection of 11-nor-Δ^9-THC-9-carboxylic acid in urine. J Anal Toxicol 2002; 26: 460–463.
23. Burrows DL, Nicolaides A, Rice PJ, Duforc M, Johnson DA, Ferslew KE. Papain: a novel urine adulterant. J Anal Toxicol 2005; 29: 275–295.
24. Dasgupta A, Wahed A, Wells A. Rapid spot tests for detecting the presence of adulterants in urine specimens submitted for drug testing. Am J Clin Pathol 2002; 117: 325–329.
25. Freslew KE, Hagardorn AN, Roberts TA. Capillary ion electrophoresis of endogenous anions and anionic adulterants in human urine. J Forensic Sci 2001; 46: 615–626.
26. Ferslew KE, Nicolaides AN, Robert TA. Determination of chromate adulteration of human urine by automated colorimetric and capillary ion electrophoretic analyses. J Anal Toxicol 2003; 27: 36–39.
27. Paul BD. Six spectrometric methods for detection of oxidants in urine: implication in differentiation of normal and adulterated urine. J Anal Toxicol 2004; 28: 599–608.
28. Singh J, Elberlind JA, Hemphill DG, Holmstrom J. The measurement of nitrite in adulterated urine samples by high performance ion chromatography. J Anal Toxicol 1999; 23: 137–140.
29. Kinkennon AE, Black DL, Robert TA, Stout PR. Analysis of nitrite in adulterated urine samples by capillary electrophoresis. J Forensic Sci 2004; 49: 1094–1100.
30. Valtier S, Cody JT. A procedure for the detection of Stealth adulterant in urine samples. Clin Lab Sci 2002; 15: 111–115.
31. Wu A, Schmalz J, Bennett W. Identification of Urin-Aid adulterated urine specimens by fluorometric analysis [Letter]. Clin Chem 1994; 40: 845–846.
32. King EJ. Performance of AdultaCheck 4 test strips for the detection of adulteration at the point of collection of urine specimen used for drugs of abuse testing. J Anal Toxicol 1999; 72 [Letter to the editor].
33. Peace MR, Tarnai LD. Performance evaluation of three on-site adulteration detection devices for urine specimens. J Anal Toxicol 2002; 26: 464–470.
34. King EJ. Performance of AdultaCheck 4 test stripes for the detection of adulteration at the point of collection of urine specimens used for drugs of abuse testing. J Anal Toxicol 1999; 23: 72.

35. Dasgupta A, Chughtai O, Hannah C, Davis B, Wells A. Comparison of spot tests with AdultaCheck 6 and Intect 7 urine test strips for detecting the presence of adulterants in urine specimens. Clin Chem Acta 2004; 34: 19–25.
36. Jones JT, Esposito FM. An assay evaluation of the methylene blue method for the detection of anionic surfactants in urine. J Anal Toxicol 2000; 24: 323–327.
37. MRO Case Studies (Health and Human Services of the US Government) 2005: (http://workplace.samhsa.gov/DrugTesting/Files_Drug_Testing/MROs/MRO%20Case%20 Studies%20-%20Ferbruary%202005.pdf)

Chapter 6
Adulterating Hair, Oral Fluid, and Sweat Specimens for Drug Testing

Abstract Although the majority of drug testings are performed using urine specimens, more recently drug testing in alternative specimens such as hair, oral fluid, and sweat have been gaining popularity. One advantage of performing drug testing using these alternative specimens is that it is extremely difficult for the donor to adulterate the specimen as occurs with urine drug testing when the urine collection process is not supervised. Nevertheless, there are commercially available shampoos and hair cleaners which claim to wash out drugs from hair follicles. In addition, mouthwashes are available to pass drug testing using oral fluid specimens. Unlike various urinary adulterants which are effective in masking some drug testing, most of the products marketed for cheating drug tests involving hair, oral fluid, and sweat are ineffective.

Keywords Hair testing · Oral fluid testing · Sweat testing

1 Introduction

Although approximately 90% of all workplace drug testings are performed using urine specimens, drug testing using alternative specimens such as hair, oral fluid, and sweat are gaining popularity for several reasons. In contrast to urine specimens where most drugs can be detected only for 2–3 days, in hair specimens, drugs can be detected for months. Monitoring drugs in an oral fluid specimen can determine very recent abuse of a drug. Measuring drugs in oral fluid is gaining importance in several countries to evaluate impairment in drivers. In December 2004, a new legislative framework for random drug screening of drivers modeled on successful random alcohol screening methodology was instituted in Victoria, Australia. The law prohibits driving under influence of methamphetamine, 3,4-methylenedioxymethamphetamine (MDMA) and marijuana (delta-9-tetrahydrocannabinol, THC). This is enforced by police who have legislative authority to test drivers randomly for these drugs using oral fluid specimens [1]. After the implementation, 13,175 roadside drug tests were performed in the first year. On-site screening was conducted by the police using DrugWipe, while the

A. Dasgupta, *Beating Drug Tests and Defending Positive Results*,
DOI 10.1007/978-1-60761-527-9_6, © Springer Science+Business Media, LLC 2010

driver was still in the vehicle and, if positive, a second test was performed also using oral fluid and RapiScan instrument. Presumptive positive cases were then sent to the laboratory for testing methamphetamine, MDMA and THC using limits of quantitation of 5, 5 and 2 ng/mL, respectively. These roadside testings yielded 313 positive cases following GC/MS confirmation. These comprised 269 cases of positive methamphetamine, 118 cases of positive MDMA and 87 cases of positive THC [2].

Hair testing is very useful to determine repeated or chronic drug use. Hair testing is now also implemented in workplace drug testing as well as on legal cases. Hair analysis is not only useful to determine drug abuse and abuse of prescription drugs but also to determine exposure to pesticides, heavy metals, organic pollutants and other substances [3].

Detailed discussion on methodologies employed for drug testing in alternative specimens is beyond the scope of this book. This chapter describes how people try to beat drug testing using alternative specimens and presents a brief discussion on drug testing in each alternative matrix.

2 Hair Drug Testing

Hair analysis is useful when assessment of drug abuse over a broader time window is desired because in hair the drugs can be detected for many days to many years. Hair grows at an average rate of 0.5–1 cm per month and testing of hair specimens is useful for pre-employment, random drug screen, return to duty or follow-up testing. However, it takes seven to ten days for drug/metabolite to be incorporated in hair and hair testing has no value in assessing recent exposure to a drug. Drug is incorporated in hair from blood capillaries and also from sweat and sebum. Once incorporated in the hair shaft, under good conditions such as protection from light, heat and moisture, the drugs are stable for hundreds of years. As early as 1979, using radioimmunoassay, Baumgartner et al. reported the detection of morphine in hair [4]. Since then, a number of drugs including amphetamines, cocaine, cannabinoids and phencyclidine have been reported to incorporate in hair. In addition, fetal hair has been used to detect maternal drug abuse during pregnancy.

Hair sample collection is not standardized and varies significantly among collection facilities and laboratories. Most testing facilities recommend collecting specimens from the back of the head called the vertex posterior. Hair in this area has less variability in growth and number of hairs in the growth phase and are less influenced by age and sex [5]. Usually a 150- to 300-mg sample is sufficient for screening and confirmation of drugs of abuse. SAMHSA proposes use of $\sim$1.5-inch long hairs which represent a time period of $\sim$60–90 days. For analysis, drugs if present in the hair specimen must be extracted. Prior to that, washing of hair specimens to remove environmental contamination is necessary. Use of various aqueous solvents for extraction of drugs from hair has been reported in the literature, but in general organic solvents perform better than aqueous solvents for extraction of drugs from hair specimens. After extraction, specimens can be screened by appropriate immunoassays and confirmed by gas chromatography-mass spectrometry (GC/MS) or liquid chromatography-mass spectrometry (LC/MS) except that much higher sensitivities are needed for drug analysis in hair specimens compared to urine drug testing. Recommended screening and cut-off levels of various drugs in hair specimens as recommended by the SAMHSA are given in Table 6.1.

2.1 Hair Color and Incorporation of Drugs

Melanin that determines hair color is a polyanionic polymer of eumelanin and pheomelanin. Eumelanin concentration is highest in black colored hair whereas red hair has the highest concentration of pheomelanin. White hairs do not have melanin. It has been hypothesized that incorporation of various drugs into hair depends on the concentration of melanin. However, there are conflicting reports in the literature as to whether there is any significant difference between hair color as well as ethnicity and incorporation of drugs into hair.

Kronstrand et al. measured methamphetamine and amphetamine levels in patients receiving selegiline, the drug which metabolizes to methamphetamine and amphetamine. Methamphetamine and amphetamine in hair showed preference for pigmented hairs over white hair [6]. Goldberger et al. found higher concentrations of cocaine in hair of people of African origin compared to the Caucasoid group [7]. In contrast, Schaffer et al. [8] studied cocaine incorporation in blonde, auburn, brown and black hair, and did not observe any difference between hair specimens of different colors. However, when hair was permed, there was an increase in cocaine uptake [8]. A study on 1,852 applicants for employment that classified themselves as "black" or "white" showed no significant difference between hair and urine drug test results for these two classes [9].

2.2 Environmental Contamination and Hair Drug Testing

Environmental exposure to drugs may contaminate hair specimens and drug users often defend positive hair testing results by claiming passive exposure to drugs. Therefore, washing of hair specimens prior to extraction of drugs is essential to produce valid results. In a recent study using 90 children between 18 months and 5 years old attending the emergency room of Hospital del Mar in Barcelona, Spain, the authors using GC/MS confirmed the presence of cocaine (range: 0.2–5.96 ng/mg of hair) in 21 children. One hair specimen was positive for MDMA and another positive for opiate. In 88% of positive cases cocaine was also found in the hair of accompanying parents. Therefore this unsuspected exposure of cocaine in such children can be confirmed using hair analysis [10]. In another study using Canadian children, the authors observed a significant correlation between cocaine concentrations in the hair of infants and their caregivers based on a study of 19 child-caregiver pairs. There was no such correlation in older children. The authors concluded that measurement of cocaine hair concentrations can allow estimation of the degree of

Table 6.1 SAMHSA-proposed initial screen and confirmation cut-off concentration of drugs of abuse in hair, oral fluid, and saliva

Specimen	Screen test cut-off level	Confirmation test cut-off level
Hair		
Marijuana metabolite	1 pg/mg	0.05 pg/mL
Cocaine metabolite	500 pg/mg	50 pg/mg
Opiate metabolite	200 pg/mg	N/A
Codeine	N/A	200 pg/mg
Morphine	N/A	200 pg/mg
Phencyclidine	300 pg/mg	200 pg/mg
Amphetamine/methamphetamine[a]	500	300 pg/mg
MDMA	500	300 pg/mg
MDA	N/A	300 pg/mg
MDEA	N/A	300 pg/mg
Oral fluid		
Marijuana or metabolite	4 ng/mL	2 ng/mL (THC)
Cocaine metabolite	20 ng/mL	8 ng/mL
Opiate metabolite	40	N/A
Morphine	N/A	40 ng/mL
Codeine	N/A	40 ng/mL
6-Monoacetylmorphine	N/A	40 ng/mL
Phencyclidine	10 ng/mL	10 ng/mL
Amphetamine/methamphetamine[a]	50	50 ng/mL
MDMA	50	50 ng/mL
MDA	N/A	50 ng/mL
MDEA	N/A	50 ng/mL
Sweat patch		
Marijuana	4 ng/patch	1 ng/patch
Cocaine metabolite	25 ng/patch	25 ng/patch
Opiate metabolite	25	N/A
Morphine	N/A	25 ng/patch
Codeine	N/A	25 ng/patch
6-Monoacetylmorphine	N/A	25 ng/patch
Phencyclidine	20 ng/patch	20 ng/patch
Amphetamine/methamphetamine[a]	25 ng/patch	25 ng/patch
MDMA	25 ng/patch	25 ng/patch
MDA	N/A	25 ng/patch
MDEA	N/A	25 ng/patch

Source: Federal Register Vol 69, No 71, Tuesday April 13th, 2004, Page 19697
[a]Methamphetamine is the target analyte for amphetamine screen. However, if methamphetamine is confirmed by GC/MS, amphetamine must be present in the specimen to identify the specimen as positive for amphetamines
MDMA: 3,4-Methylenedioxymethamphetamine
MDA: 3,4-Methylenedioxyamphetamine
MDEA: 3,4-Methylenedioxyethylamphetamine.

environmental drug exposure in young children [11]. Detection of cocaine metabolites may differentiate active use of cocaine from external contamination. Koren et al. showed that pyrolysis of crack results in accumulation of cocaine in hair, but not its metabolite benzoylecgonine [12]. On the other hand, in cocaine abusers both cocaine and benzoylecgonine are detectable in hair. Washing may not remove all cocaine in hair accumulated from extensive environmental exposure. On the other hand, if intense washing procedures are used, they can lead to removal of drugs from hair, thus raising the chance of false negative results [13,14].

Certain shampoos contain significant amounts (1–3%) of cannabinoids including THC, cannabidiol (CBD) and cannabinol (CBN). To explore the possibility of false positive results due to the use of Cannabio shampoo, three subjects washed their hair with Cannabio shampoo once daily for 2 weeks [15]. In the case of passive marijuana smoke, the hair specimen should only contain the parent drug (THC) but not the marijuana metabolite THC–COOH (11-nor-Δ^9-tetrahydrocannabinol-9-carboxylic acid). Uhl and Sachs reported a case where a male subject used marijuana but the female subject was exposed to passive smoke. The hair sample from the male subject tested positive for marijuana metabolite THC–COOH but the female subject only tested positive for the presence of THC [16]. Like cocaine and cannabinoids, the questions about external contamination by PCP have been raised. To rule out passive exposure, the detection of PCP metabolites may be helpful Overall, the use of effective wash procedures, appropriate cut-offs and metabolite analyses should differentiate between drug abuse versus passive exposure to a drug in hair analysis.

2.3 *Adulteration of Hair Specimens*

Since hairs are generally collected under direct supervision, the chances of adulteration during sample collection are minimal. However, treatment of hair before sample collection can occur and may affect the results. There are a number of products available on the Internet which guarantee to beat the hair drug test. Although a number of these products claim to work 100%, there is little scientific evidence that any of these products really work. For example, the Internet site for Ultra Clean Shampoo claims "Hair Purifying Shampoo is designed for extremely swift yet elegant removal of all toxin residues. Within 10 min, you will be in the 'Clean Zone' for up to 4 h. It is safe for the scalp and all hair types." Rohrich et al. investigated the effect of Ultra Clean on removing tetrahydrocannabinol (THC), cocaine, amphetamine, 3,4-methylenedioxyamphetamine (MDA), 3,4-methylenedioxymethamphetamine (MDMA), 3,4-methylenedioxyethylamphetamine (MDE), heroin, 6-monoacetylmorphine (6-MAM), morphine, codeine, dihydrocodeine and methadone from hair samples. In this study, postmortem hair samples from subjects with known histories of drug abuse were used and specimens were analyzed either without any treatment or after treating with Ultra Clean shampoo. Although none of the specimens tested negative after treatment with the shampoo, there was a slight decrease in drug concentrations compared to untreated specimens. The authors concluded that a single use of Ultra Clean did not sufficiently remove these drugs to cause negative results [17].

3 Oral Fluid Testing for Abused Drugs

Oral fluid is easy to collect under direct supervision without the need for a special sample collection facility. In addition, oral fluid testing is capable of indicating recent drug use and the concentrations of drugs in oral fluid correlate well with blood concentrations. Concentrations of drugs in oral fluid are affected by many factors including oral fluid volume, plasma pH, oral fluid pH, drug ionization and protein binding. Oral fluid is slightly acidic with a pH of approximately 5.5 but may go up to 8 depending on the flow of oral fluid. The drugs in oral fluid mostly exist in free form. Therefore the change in pH changes the drug concentration in oral fluid due to change in drug ionization and thus diffusion of drugs into oral fluid from blood. Oral fluid contains approximately 90% water and 10% solutes such as electrolytes, amylase, glucose, urea and proteins. Drugs are incorporated into oral fluid by passive diffusion, ultrafiltration and secretion. In addition, if a drug is taken orally or smoked, it can also be incorporated into oral fluid.

For the collection of oral fluid, the donor should be supervised for 10–20 min prior to sample collection and should not be allowed to put anything in his/her mouth during this period. Stimulation of oral fluid production can be achieved through sucking sour candy or citric acid crystals or by chewing on an inert material such as Teflon. Materials such as Para film absorb lipophilic drugs and should not be used for oral fluid stimulation. Commercial oral fluid collectors have stimulator and absorbent pads in a single unit. Samples collected using these collection devices generally provide higher quality sample (cleaner and high volume) than direct spitting.

Once the oral fluid is collected, it can be tested on-site or in the laboratory. The performance of on-site devices varies significantly, and thus a specific on-site device should be evaluated for a specific need. One study that compared several on-site devices found that most devices perform well for methamphetamine and opiates but not for cannabinoids. The performance for cocaine and amphetamine varied between devices [18]. In another study, the point-of-collection devices performed well for opiates and amphetamines but testing for cocaine and delta-9-tetrahydrocannibinol (THC) showed wide variations [19].

When sending samples to a laboratory for testing it is important that the sample should be handled and shipped properly to avoid sample deterioration, and the chain of custody regulations must be followed. Most of the drugs are stable for several days at 4 °C or at room temperature in oral fluid. Ventura et al. studied the stability of various drugs in oral fluid collection devices and concluded that, on average, in 48–72 h, 9–12% of 6-monocaetylmorphine was converted into morphine, between 26% and 41% cocaine into benzoylecgonine, and good recoveries were observed for marijuana (THC) [20]. The screening and confirmation cut-off concentrations of various drugs in oral fluid are given in Table 6.1. The laboratory screening for abused drugs in oral fluid is generally performed by immunoassays, followed by confirmation of positive samples using gas chromatography-mass spectrometry (GC–MS) [21]. More recently, several methods using liquid chromatography combined with tandem mass spectrometry have been reported in the literature for analysis of drug of abuse in oral fluid specimens [22].

In general, oral fluid and blood have a higher concentration of parent drugs compared to urine, whereas urine has a higher concentration of drug metabolites. Therefore, parent drugs are assayed in oral fluid but, in order to differentiate between drug abuse and passive exposure, measurement of drug metabolite in oral fluid is also recommended. Besides common drugs of abuse such as amphetamines, barbiturates, benzodiazepines, cocaine, cannabinoids, gamma-hydroxybutyrate (GHB), opiates, and PCP, the presence of many other drugs have been reported in oral fluid. These drugs include caffeine, carbamazepine, cisplatin, cyclosporine, digoxin, ethosuximide, irinotecan, lithium, methadone, metoprolol, nicotine, oxprenolol, paracetamol, phenytoin, primidone, procainamide, quinine, sulfanilamide, theophylline, and tolbutamide [23].

3.1 Adulteration of Oral Fluid

A number of adulterants are available on the Internet and claim to beat the drug test. Many studies investigated the effect of these adulterants on drug testing in oral fluid specimens. Wong et al. investigated the effects of various adulterants and foodstuffs on the Oratect device and found that these products do not interfere in the testing. In addition, two commercially available adulterant products such as Clear Choice and Fizzy Flush manufactured by Health Tech (Atlanta, GA) contained potassium, sodium, creatinine monohydrate, vitamin B2, and proprietary ingredients including uva, ursi, dandelion, cranberry, ginkgo biloba, and stevia. Each box contains two 5-mg effervescent tablets. To use, one tablet must be dissolved in 300 mL of water and then the solution must be swished in the mouth for 10 s followed by swallowing it. The process must be repeated until the entire amount is consumed. The solution appeared yellowish brown, smelled like orange juice and had a bittersweet taste. Black particles were also observed to be settled at the bottom. The author also tested another adulterant, "Spit n Kleen Mouthwash." In addition the authors also tested commercially available Cool Mint Listerine mouthwash. In a food interference study, three groups of volunteers each consumed a full course of ethnic dishes including Mexican beef Burritos, Vietnamese Pho noodles and the American continental food of fried chicken or beef. The authors concluded that these adulteration products had no effect in destroying the drug molecules or changing the pH of the oral fluid. The effect of these adulterants was through washing of the oral cavity and was not different from a common mouthwash. In addition, consumption of ethnic or American food does not interfere with oral fluid testing [24]. In another study, a series of potential interfering substances (alcohol, hard candy, chewing gum, coffee, tea, orange juice, water, smoking, and mouthwash) on oral fluid were evaluated on Cozart microplate EIA for opiates, and no effect of these substances was observed [25]. Overall, there is no scientific evidence that these adulterants really work. However to minimize questions of adulteration, several measures are recommended. SAMSHA recommends the measurement of human IgG in oral fluid samples. Absence of human IgG in the sample suggests sample adulteration.

4 Sweat Testing

Sweat testing provides a convenient and virtually non-invasive method for continuous monitoring of drug abuse and is currently used to monitor drug abstinence in criminal justice and drug rehabilitation programs. Because a sweat collection patch can be put on the body for a period of 1–2 weeks, continuous monitoring of drug abuse in a person can be determined by sweat testing and it is an alternative to urine drug testing where multiple specimens must be collected to assess drug abuse of an individual over such a period. Passive diffusion is considered to be the primary mechanism of drug incorporation into sweat.

Sweat is collected on a patch that is affixed to the upper arm or torso like a band-aid. Several devices are available for sweat collection. One such device called PharmChek (PharmChem Inc., Haltom City, TX) is FDA (Federal Drug Administration) approved and has been used in a number of studies. The patch has an absorbent pad covered by a protective membrane similar to that of a band-aid. The protective membrane prevents external contamination of the absorbent pad. Before applying the pad, the subject's skin should be thoroughly cleaned by an organic solvent such as isopropanol to remove any dirt, skin oils, or skin care products such as lotions and creams. This also helps in removing any external drug contamination. The sweat patches are waterproof, tamper resistant, and comfortable to wear. Taking a shower or swimming with the patch on is allowed. Once the sweat has been collected, the patch is removed and sent to a laboratory for drug testing. There is no point of collection device available for sweat testing. In the laboratory the adsorbent pad is removed and soaked and then shaken in a buffer in order to elute drugs. The eluent is tested for drugs by immunoassays or chromatographic techniques. The cut-off concentrations for individual drugs in sweat specimens are significantly lower than the cut-off values in urine specimens (Table 6.1).

Amphetamines and other sympathomimetic drugs have been detected in sweat including the designer drug 3,4-methylenedioxymethamphetamine (MDMA). Sweat patches have also been used in the detection of cannabinoids in sweat [26]. Cocaine and its metabolites have also been detected in sweat. In contrast to urine, sweat primarily contains the parent drug cocaine, and ecgonine methyl ester [27]. In addition to the above-mentioned drugs, various other drugs and their metabolites, including heroin, 6-monoacetylmorphine, morphine, codeine, hydrocodone, methadone, 2-ethylidene-1,5-dimethyl-3,3-diphenylpyrrolidine (EDDP), phencyclidine, and clozapine, have been detected in sweat.

4.1 Adulteration Issues

Some people may develop an allergic reaction and inflammation after putting on a sweat patch. Sweat is slightly acidic with an average pH of ~5.8. During exercise the pH of sweat increases to an average of 6.4, and may affect the drug diffusion. Questions have been raised about the possibility of sweat patch adulteration. Once the patch has been properly applied, it is difficult to contaminate as the outer polyurethane layer is impermeable to molecules larger than water. The studies have shown that the contaminants applied to the outer layer do not reach the collection pad. In one study the effect of 18 adulterants on enzyme immunoassay and GC–MS for opiates was investigated. In this study, the sweat patches were spiked with adulterants and air dried. The patches were then spiked with heroin, codeine or morphine and incubated at 37 °C for 7 days. Most of the adulterants tested did not cause any significant effect. Also, exposure of the skin to many of these adulterants causes visible irritation, making use of these adulterants unlikely. However, injecting adulterants using a hypodermic needle is a possibility. Therefore, it is recommended that, before analysis, the outside layer of the patch be examined against the light for possible tampering [28].

5 Conclusions

Drug testing in alternative specimens is gaining acceptance in workplace drug testing and has several advantages over conventional urine drug testing. In addition, adulteration of hair, oral fluid, or sweat specimens is more difficult than adulteration of urine specimens. In contrast to urine drug testing, where several adulterants including strong oxidizing agents (nitrite and chromate) can destroy certain drug/metabolite thus causing false negative results in screening and GC/MS confirmation, attempted adulteration of hair, oral fluid, or sweat specimens using various commercially available adulterants are virtually ineffective.

References

1. Boorman M, Owens K. The Victorian legislative framework for the random testing drivers at the roadside for the presence of illicit drugs: an evaluation of the characteristics of drivers detected from 2004 to 2006. Traffic Inj Prev 2009; 10: 16–22.
2. Drummer OH, Gerostamoulos D, Chu M, Swann P et al. Drugs in oral fluid in randomly selected drivers. Forensic Sci Int 2007; 170: 105–110.
3. Boumba VA, Ziavrou KS, Vougioulakis T. Hair analysis as a biological indicator of drug use, drug abuse or chronic exposure ti environmental toxins. Int J Toxicol 2006; 25: 143–163.
4. Baumgartner AM, Jones PF, Baumgartner WA, Black CT. Radioimmunoassay of hair for determining opiate-abuse histories. J Nucl Med 1979; 20: 748–752.
5. Kintz P. Value of hair analysis in postmortem toxicology. Forensic Sci Int 2004; 142: 127–134.
6. Kronstrand R, Ahlner J, Dizdar N, Larson G. Quantitative analysis of desmethylselegiline, methamphetamine, and amphetamine in hair and plasma from Parkinson patients on long-term selegiline medication. J Anal Toxicol 2003; 27: 135–141.
7. Goldberger BA, Darraj AG, Caplan YH, Cone EJ. Detection of methadone, methadone metabolites, and other illicit drugs of abuse in hair of methadone-treatment subjects. J Anal Toxicol 1998; 22: 526–530.

8. Schaffer M, Hill V, Cairns T. Hair analysis for cocaine: the requirement for effective wash procedures and effects of drug concentration and hair porosity in contamination and decontamination. J Anal Toxicol 2005; 29: 319–326.
9. Hoffman BH. Analysis of race effects on drug-test results. J Occup Environ Med 1999; 41: 612–614.
10. Joya X, Papaseit E, Civit E, Pellegrini M et al. Unsuspected exposure to cocaine in preschool children from a Mediterranean city detected by hair analysis. Ther Drug Monit 2009 [E-pub ahead of print].
11. Garcia-Bournissen F, Nesterenko M, Karasjov T, Koren G. Passive environmental exposure to cocaine in Canadian children. Paediatr Drugs 2009; 11: 30–32.
12. Koren G, Klein J, Forman R, Graham K. Hair analysis of cocaine: differentiation between systemic exposure and external contamination. J Clin Pharmacol 1992; 32: 671–675.
13. Romano G, Barbera N, Lombardo I. Hair testing for drugs of abuse: evaluation of external cocaine contamination and risk of false positives. Forensic Sci Int 2001; 123: 119–129.
14. Paulsen RB, Wilkins DG, Slawson MH, Shaw K, Rollins DE. Effect of four laboratory decontamination procedures on the quantitative determination of cocaine and metabolites in hair by HPLC-MS. J Anal Toxicol 2001; 25: 490–496.
15. Cirimele V, Kintz P, Jamey C, Ludes B. Are cannabinoids detected in hair after washing with Cannabio shampoo?. J Anal Toxicol 1999; 23: 349–351.
16. Uhl M, Sachs H. Cannabinoids in hair: strategy to prove marijuana/hashish consumption. Forensic Sci Int 2004; 145: 143–147.
17. Rohrich J, Zorntlein S, Potsch L, Skopp G, Becker J. Effect of the shampoo Ultra Clean on drug concentrations in human hair. Int J Legal Med 2000; 113: 102–106.
18. Walsh JM, Flegel R, Crouch DJ, Cangianelli L, Baudys J. An evaluation of rapid point-of-collection oral fluid drug-testing devices. J Anal Toxicol 2003; 27: 429–439.
19. Walsh JM, Crouch DJ, Danaceau JP, Cangianelli L, Liddicoat L, Adkins R. Evaluation of ten oral fluid point-of-collection drug-testing devices. J Anal Toxicol 2007; 31: 44–54.
20. Ventura M, Pichini S, Ventura R, Leal S et al. Stability of drugs of abuse in oral fluid collection devices with purpose of external quality assessment schemes. Ther Drug Monit 2009; 31: 277–280.
21. Kintz P, Brunet B, Muller JF, Serra W et al.. Evaluation of the Cozart DDVS test for cannabis in oral fluid. Ther Drug Monit 2009; 31: 131–134.
22. Kala V, Harris SE, Freijo TD, Gerlich S. Validation of analysis of amphetamine, opiates, phencyclidine, cocaine, benzoylecgonine in oral fluids by liquid chromatography-tandem mass spectrometry. J Anal Toxicol 2008; 32: 605–611.
23. Kaufman E, Lamster IB. The diagnostic applications of oral fluid—a review. Crit Rev Oral Biol Med 2002; 13: 197–212.
24. Wong RC, Tran M, Tung JK. Oral fluid drug tests: effects of adulterants and foodstuffs. Forensic Sci Int 2005; 150: 175–180.
25. Cooper G, Wilson L, Reid C, Baldwin D, Hand C, Spiehler V. Validation of the Cozart microplate EIA for analysis of opiates in oral fluid. Forensic Sci Int 2005; 154: 240–246.
26. Saito T, Wtsadik A, Scheidweiler KB, Fortner N, Takeichi S, Huestis MA. Validated gas chromatographic-negative ion chemical ionization mass spectrometric method for delta(9)-tetrahydrocannabinol in sweat patches. Clin Chem 2004; 50: 2083–2090.
27. Kacinko SL, Barnes AJ, Schwilke EW, Cone EJ, Moolchan ET, Huestis MA. Disposition of cocaine and its metabolites in human sweat after controlled cocaine administration. Clin Chem 2005; 51: 2085–2094.
28. Fogerson R, Schoendorfer D, Fay J, Spiehler V. Qualitative detection of opiates in sweat by EIA and GC-MS. J Anal Toxicol 1997; 21: 451–458.

Chapter 7
Defending Positive Opiate and Marijuana Test Results

Abstract The best defense for a positive opiate test result is the claim of eating poppy seed containing food prior to the urine drug test. Although eating poppy seed containing food may result in a positive morphine or codeine level in the urine specimen, semisynthetic opiates such as oxycodone, hydromorphone, hydrocodone, and oxycodone, as well as the widely abused drug heroin, are not found in poppy seeds, and the presence of any one of these compounds in the specimen is not consistent with ingestion of poppy seed containing food. Although heroin has a very short half-life, confirmation of 6-acetylmorphine is consistent with heroin abuse and not related to eating poppy seed containing food. Although passive inhalation of marijuana is a popular defense against confirmed marijuana test results, published papers indicate that such passive inhalation is not sufficient to reach the cut-off level of marijuana screening. Similarly, ingestion of hemp oil, which may contain very small amount of marijuana, is unlikely to cause a positive drug test. However, ingestion of synthetic marijuana, Marinol, should cause a positive marijuana result.

Keywords Defending positive test · Hemp · Poppy seed

1 Introduction

Although opium is illegal, poppy seeds are legally sold in the United States for consumption in various foods. Poppy seed muffins, poppy seed breads, and poppy seed cakes are popular foods for breakfasts and snacks. Much higher amounts of poppy seeds are used in various ethnic cooking. In Indian cooking, poppy seeds are ground into paste and are used for thickening of gravy. Poppy seeds are also used in noodle, fish, and vegetable dishes in German, Slavic and Jewish cooking. Such ethnic dishes contain more poppy seeds than poppy seed muffins or cakes and after consumption of such dishes much higher urinary opiate level is expected. Poppy plants are not grown in the United States and poppy seeds are imported from various countries. The opium content of poppy seed depends on the particular breed of the plant and

A. Dasgupta, *Beating Drug Tests and Defending Positive Results*,

DOI 10.1007/978-1-60761-527-9_7,

may vary widely. Hemp products contain small amounts of marijuana but consumption of a reasonable amount of hemp oil should not produce a positive marijuana test result in the urine specimen. Similarly, passive inhalation of marijuana is unlikely to cause a positive test result.

2 Poppy Seeds and Opium

Poppy plants (*P. somniferum, P. paeoniflorum, P. giganteum*) are annual plants that can grow almost anywhere but are mostly found in India, Turkey, Afghanistan, Iran, China, Mediterranean regions, and some European countries. Of all the different species, *Papaverus somniferum* is the most popular due to both its beautiful flowers and its seeds which are used for making muffins, baking breads, and other purposes. Opium is found in the latex (a milky fluid) collected from immature seed capsules of poppy plants 1–3 weeks after flowering by incision of green seed pods. More than 20 alkaloids have been isolated from *Papaverus somniferum* out of which three alkaloids – morphine, codeine, and noscapine (antitussive) – are used in therapy. Thebaine is a biosynthetic intermediate of the morphine pathway which is used by the pharmaceutical industry for synthesis of oxycodone and opiate antagonist naloxone [1]. Morphine, codeine, and thebaine are narcotic alkaloids found in opium whereas other alkaloids such as papaverine, noscapine, and narcotine are non-narcotic alkaloids.

Opium and its constituent chemicals are listed as Schedule II drugs while heroin, a semi-synthetic opiate, is a Schedule I drug. Opium poppies for legal pharmaceutical purposes are grown in various countries under government license but very few are produced in the United States. The countries which can legally export crude opium to the United States include India, Turkey, Spain, France, Poland, Hungary, and Australia. India is the largest exporter of opium to the legal pharmaceutical markets of the world. Growing opium poppies (*Papaverus somniferum*) is currently illegal in the United States and recently it has become more and more dangerous to have a patch of them growing in your backyard. The sale of poppy seed from *Papaverus somniferum* is banned in Singapore and Saudi Arabia.

2.1 Opium Content of Various Poppy Seeds

The morphine and codeine contents of poppy seeds vary widely. The morphine content of the Australian poppy seeds ranges from 90 to 200 μg of morphine per gram of poppy seed while Dutch and Turkish poppy seed contain only 4–5 μg of morphine per gram of poppy seed [1–4]. Pelders et al. studied morphine and codeine content of poppy seeds originating from Australia, Hungary, Czech Republic, Spain, Turkey, and Netherlands [3]. The authors found the highest amount of morphine and codeine in poppy seeds imported from Spain (Table 7.1). In general there is a wide variation of morphine and codeine content in commercially available poppy seeds [4,5].

Table 7.1 Typical morphine and codeine content of various poppy seeds originated from different countries

Country of origin of poppy seed	Morphine (μg/g of seed)	Codeine (μg/g of seed)	Reference
Australia	90	6.5	3
Australia	325	NR	4
Hungary	46	3.7	3
Hungary	6.9	NR	5
Spain	251	57.1	3
Netherlands	4	0.4	3
Czech Republic	2	0.5	3
Turkey	5	1.2	3
Turkey	27	15.5	3
Denmark	8.4	NR	5
Hungary	44	NR	13
Denmark	10	NR	13
Australia	200	NR	13
Spain	60	NR	13

NR: Not reported

2.2 Poppy Seed and Allergy

Although very rare, severe allergic reaction may occur after consumption of poppy seed containing food. Individuals who are allergic to pollen or nuts are susceptible to allergic reaction after exposure to poppy seeds. Keskin and Sekerel reported the case of a 16-year-old boy who developed erythema and angioedema, conjunctivitis and dyspnea due to inhalation of poppy seeds. Skin-prick tests were positive for poppy seeds, hazelnuts and chickpeas and specific IgE related to poppy seed was also identified [6]. Another report describes the case of a 17-year-old boy who was admitted to hospital with a history of a generalized reaction soon after eating a poppy seed cake. The reaction consisted of acute abdominal pain which was quickly followed by diffuse urticaria and low blood pressure (70/45). After treatment with adrenaline and corticosteroids, his symptoms were improved but about 1 h afterwards he complained again of severe abdominal pains, requiring a new dose of adrenaline. A couple of weeks later he felt a tingling and burning sensation in his mouth after eating cheesecake which was kept close to poppy seeds. Eventually poppy seed specific IgE was detected in his blood [7].

2.3 Opiate Level After Consumption of Poppy Tea (Opium Tea)

Poppy tea is a narcotic analgesic tea which is brewed from dried *Papaverus somniferum* plants, seed pods, or seeds. The tea is usually bitter in taste and the flavor is sometimes improved by mixing it with coffee, honey, or lemon juice. The effects of drinking this tea may start as early as 30 min after consumption and may last for several hours because of its high opiate content compared to eating poppy seed containing food where opiate intake is very low and not enough to cause euphoria. Drinking poppy tea may cause opiate addiction [8]. In Denmark it is illegal to grow opium poppy for the production of poppy seeds, but until 1986 poppy trees could be grown for decoration purposes. The morphine content of opium may be up to 24% prepared from Danish poppy. Opium tea was widely abused in Denmark by drug addicts and, between 1982 and 1985, seven fatalities occurred in Denmark solely or partly due to the consumption of opium poppies [9].

Significant amounts of morphine may be found in blood and urine of subjects consuming poppy tea. A baker consumed poppy tea prepared from seeds and experienced tonic-clonic seizure and delirium. His business partner said that he was purchasing 25 kg of poppy seeds per week whereas only 3 kg were required for the bakery. The concentration of morphine in his blood was almost 3.0 mg/L. The patient admitted drinking about 2 L of poppy tea made from 4 kg of seeds. When a typical tea was prepared the morphine concentration was 0.14 mg/mL, indicating that he was consuming approximately 280 mg morphine a day [10]. Van Thuyne et al. reported that the morphine content of tea prepared from two specimens of a different species of poppy (*Papaveris fructus*) was 10.4 and 31.5 μg/mL, which was consumed by five subjects. Maximum urinary concentration of morphine ranged from 4.3 μg/mL (4,300 ng/mL) and 7.4 μg/mL (7,400 ng/mL) [11].

2.4 Consumption of Poppy Seed Containing Food and Urinary Opiates

It has been well established that eating poppy seed containing food results in urinary opiate levels over 300 ng/mL, the traditional cut-off for opiate screening using a commercially available immunoassay. In November 1998, the Federal Government (DHHS: Department of Health and Human Services) increased the screening cut-off of opiate immunoassays from 300 to 2,000 ng/mL in an attempt to eliminate false positive opiate results due to ingestion of poppy seed products. Fraser and Worth reported that, following the new guideline, codeine and morphine positive results were reduced from 7.1% positive in 1994–1996 to 2.1% in 1998 [12]. The reported values of morphine after consumption of poppy seed products varied widely with values in the range of 312–17,900 ng/mL [4,13–16]. The male volunteer (body weight 90 kg) who showed 17,900 ng/mL of morphine in urine consumed a calculated amount of 30 mg of morphine from poppy seeds in conjunction with neutral cake. Another male subject with a body weight of 75 kg showed a maximum urinary morphine level of 17,700 ng/mL after an estimated morphine intake of 20 mg. Nevertheless, after 24 h of consumption, urinary morphine levels in these subjects dropped to 300 ng/mL. When these subjects consumed poppy seed cake but not pure poppy seed with neutral cake, maximum morphine concentrations in urine were significantly lower. For example, when the volunteer with 90 kg body weight consumed poppy seed cake (calculated morphine intake 3.7 mg), the maximum urinary morphine concentration was only 1,800 ng/mL [13].

The main reason for such wide variations in reported morphine and codeine levels after consumption of poppy seed containing food is that the authors used poppy seeds imported from different countries and in some studies subjects ingested unreasonable amounts of poppy seeds. In our experience, consumption of a poppy seed muffin or a poppy seed cake results in urinary opiate levels well below 2,000 ng/mL.

According to the American Spice Trade Association, New York, Australian, Dutch and Turkish poppy seed varieties constituted 94% of the American market. In general, morphine content of Australian poppy seeds is much higher than Danish or Turkish poppy seeds. Usually poppy seeds are consumed in small quantities and popular poppy buns contain approximately 3 g of poppy seed. In one report, morphine content of 83 poppy seed samples ranged from concentrations below detection limit (<1 μg/g) to 270 μg/g. Food processing also significantly reduces morphine content of poppy seeds. For poppy cake, only 16–50% morphine and 10–50% codeine can be recovered. For poppy buns, which are baked at a higher temperature, only 3% morphine and 7% codeine are usually recovered [17]. Usually, consumption of 200.4–1,002 μg of morphine and 95.9–479.5 μg codeine (typical consumption from poppy seed containing food) resulted in urinary morphine levels between 120 and 1,270 ng/mL and codeine levels of 40–730 ng/mL [18]. Typically, morphine concentrations are higher than codeine concentrations in urine after consumption of poppy seed products. In another study, the concentrations of morphine and codeine were 2,797 and 214 ng/mL respectively in one healthy volunteer who ingested three poppy seed bagels. Opiate was present in the urine 25 h post ingestion. No opiate was present 45 h post ingestion [13].

Hayes et al. studied the effect of ingesting poppy seeds on morphine and codeine levels in urine. The poppy seeds used for this study contained 17–294 μg/g of morphine and 3–14 μg/g of codeine. The subjects ingested 40 g of poppy seeds that contained approximately 2.5 mg of morphine and 0.16 mg of codeine. The immunoassay screening of specimens by EMIT (Enzyme Multiplied Immunoassay Technique, Syva, San Jose, CA) showed a typical positive screen (>300 ng/mL cut-off) up to 24 h of ingestion of poppy seed and peak concentration of total morphine ranged from 700 to 2,600 ng/mL as measured by gas chromatography-mass spectrometry (GC/MS) [14]. Another study using poppy seeds containing 17.4–18.6 μg/g of morphine and 2.3–2.5 μg/g of codeine reported the highest morphine concentration of 4,500 ng/mL in one subject 5 h after ingestion of poppy seeds [7]. Morphine concentration of 5,880 ng/mL 6 h after ingestion of poppy seed cake in one subject was reported by Thevis et al. Other subjects who ingested poppy seed products also showed significant amounts of morphine in urine [5]. Hill et al. investigated the effect of ingesting a large amount of poppy seed on the urinary concentrations of morphine in volunteers as well as concentrations in hair. The poppy seed study was performed using Australian poppy seed because it contains the highest amount of morphine of any poppy seed available on the United States market. Ten subjects (six male, four female) ingested two servings of poppy seed pastry per week (generally on Monday and Tuesday; 8.1 mg average morphine per serving) for three weeks (total morphine consumed: 49 mg). Hair specimens were collected before and after the study. Urine specimens were collected for a 24-h period following poppy seed ingestion and then 3–5 h after subsequent ingestion of poppy seed pastry. The maximum values of urinary morphine ranged from 2,929 to 13,857 ng/mL (determined by gas chromatography-mass spectrometry). Moreover, urinary morphine levels remained above 2,000 ng/mL for as long as 10 h. Despite high urinary morphine levels, all subjects reported hair level morphine below the standard cut-off (0.04–0.48 ng of morphine/10 mg of hair, cut-off 2 ng of morphine/10 mg of hair) [4]. Typical morphine and codeine levels in urine specimens after consumption of poppy seed containing products are given in Table 7.2.

Table 7.2 Typical morphine and codeine concentrations in urine in subjects after consumption of various amounts of poppy seed products. Wide variations among subjects within same study

Sample time (post ingestion)	Morphine ng/mL	Codeine, ng/mL	Reference
3 h	2,797	214	14
22 h	676	16	14
3 h	2,635	45	15
6 h	1,460	14	15
5 h	4,500	NR	36
0–2 h	832	48	16
0–2 h	302.1	83.8	16
6 h	5,880	NR	5
6 h	10,004	NR	5
3–5 h	2,929	208	4
3–5 h	5,651	552	4
3–5 h	13,857	1,174	4
3–5 h	13,656	1,005	4
3–5 h	17,900	NR	13
3–5 h	17,700	NR	13

NR: Not reported

2.5 Consumption of Poppy Seed Containing Food and Opiate Levels in Other Matrix

Although most drug testings are performed using urine specimens, drug testing in other matrix such as blood, sweat, oral fluid, and hair is also performed. In Germany, a blood level of free morphine over10 ng/mL in a driver is considered as driving under impairment. Moeller et al. studied blood and urine morphine levels after consumption of poppy seed products. All five volunteers showed positive opiate urine drug tests (up to 2079 ng/mL by a semi-quantitative Abbott assay; urine morphine 147–1300 ng/mL by gas chromatography-mass spectrometry). No blood specimen tested positive for free morphine, but total morphine levels (after hydrolysis) of up to 24 ng/mL was observed [19]. In another study, the authors observed only trace amounts of free morphine (1–3 ng/mL) in serum after consumption of poppy seed products [20]. Currently, the suggested cut-off for oral fluid morphine is 40 ng/mL, but after consumption of poppy seed containing food, morphine concentrations above 40 ng/mL can be detected for up to 1 h post consumption in oral fluid. Using 2,000 ng/mL cut-off for opiates in urine, the authors observed that urinary specimens may test positive for opiates for up to 8 h [21].

2.6 Consumption of Poppy Seed Containing Food and Impairment

In an early study performed in Oregon, where seven volunteers each ingested 25 g of poppy seeds baked into cakes, none of the subjects were found to demonstrate any symptom of opiate impairment based on a series of standardized drug recognition evaluation tests. However, all urinary specimens screened by the EMIT opiate assay showed positive results using a cut-off concentration of 300 ng/mL [22]. Hill reported that, in their study, when subjects ate higher amounts of poppy seed products, seven out of ten subjects reported drowsiness for 1 h after taking poppy seed pastry. The effect lasted for 2–4 h [4]. However, consumption of poppy tea may be problematic because of the higher morphine content of poppy tea. Opiate addiction, opiate dependency, and hospitalization after consumption of poppy tea have been reported.

2.7 Brown Mixture and Opiate Levels

Brown mixture is used as a cold remedy and it is a prescription drug in Taiwan. Each tablet contains 2.5 mg opium powder (approximately 30 μg morphine per tablet). Following consumption of brown mixture, significant amounts of morphine and codeine can be observed in urine. In one study, after consumption of one tablet each by volunteers, the maximum urinary morphine concentration of 379 ng/mL was observed. After consumption of six tablets by volunteers, the maximum urinary concentration of morphine was 2,525 ng/mL [23].

2.8 Legal Consequence of Positive Opiate Due to Ingestion of Poppy Seed Containing Food

Positive urine opiate test results due to consumption of poppy seed containing food are well known to toxicologist and United States Bureau of Prison officials. The Bureau warns inmates that eating poppy seed may produce positive drug tests which may lead to disciplinary action. A warning is all inmates are entitled to and testing positive during supervised release may lead to an additional jail term for an individual. In general, United States courts are reluctant to give the benefit of doubt to a person using a poppy seed defense for positive opiate drug testing. Even in civil cases, where a job may be denied to a person due to a positive opiate drug result, the court is somewhere reluctant to accept poppy seed defense. Because it is not easy to challenge legally a positive opiate result due to ingestion of poppy seed containing food, it is advisable to avoid such food for at least a week before a workplace drug testing. Moreover, private employers are not obliged to use the 2,000 ng/mL cut-off level for opiate screening in urine and some of them use the old 300 ng/mL cut-off. With such a low cut-off, even eating one poppy seed bagel or cake may cause positive urine test results for several hours.

3 Marker for Poppy Seed Consumption in Urine

Heroin addicts often use a poppy seed defense to explain the presence of 6-monoacetylmorphine (6-MAM), a marker of heroin abuse, in urine. Although 6-MAM is eventually metabolized to morphine and may not be detected in all heroin abusers, the presence of the heroin-specific metabolite 6-MAM can be explained due to abuse of heroin [24]. Acetylcodeine, a synthetic byproduct present in street heroin, can also be used as a marker for heroin abuse. Detection of acetylcodeine was also reported in oral fluid collected from heroin addicts [25]. Reticuline (a precursor of opium alkaloids) is not present in heroin or poppy seed but can only be found in opium. Reticuline has been suggested as a marker to differentiate between opium and poppy seed consumption as well to differentiate between opium and pharmaceutical grade codeine use [26].

Thebaine is a natural constituent of poppy seed and there are suggestions that thebaine can be used as a marker for poppy seed consumption. In a case where morphine and codeine have been detected, the presence of thebaine would indicate poppy seed use by the subject. In one study, thebaine was detected in concentrations ranging from 2 to 91 ng/mL in volunteers after consumption of 11 g of poppy seed [27]. The elimination of thebaine (see Fig. 7.1 for chemical structure) varies widely between individuals and the absence of thebaine in a urine specimen may also be possible after consumption of poppy seed containing foods. Neither noscapine nor papaverine can be detected in urine after consumption of poppy seed containing food, but desmethylpapaverine and its glucuronide can be detected in urine specimens even 48 h after consumption of poppy seed containing food. Therefore, these compounds can also be potential markers for poppy seed use but caution should be exercised that such compounds did not originate from use of a pharmaceutic product [20].

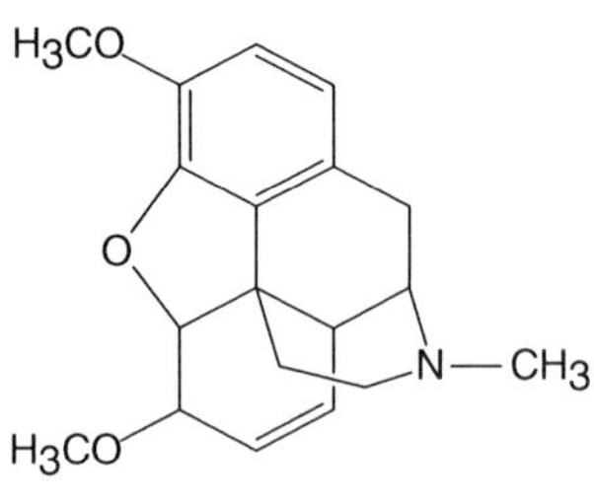

Fig. 7.1 Chemical structure of thebaine

4 Defending Positive Marijuana Results

People tested positive for marijuana usually claim passive inhalation of marijuana from attending a party. Another common defense is ingestion of hemp oil or hemp containing products. A synthetic marijuana (Δ^9-tetrahydrocannabinoid, THC), dronabinol, is available as a prescription drug under the trade name Marinol®. It is prescribed for the treatment of nausea and vomiting associated with cancer chemotherapy, appetite stimulation in AIDS patients, and the management of glaucoma. Use of Marinol should lead to a positive test for marijuana in workplace drug testing. See Chap. 10 for more detail.

4.1 Passive Inhalation of Marijuana

The cut-off limit of marijuana metabolite (11-nor-9-carboxy-Δ^9-tetrahydrocannabinol; THC−COOH) in urine is 50 ng/mL and passive inhalation of marijuana should not produce such levels in the urine. The Department of Transportation indicated that Medical Review Officers should not recognize passive drug exposure as a legitimate medical explanation for a positive test. THC released in air becomes highly dilute after mixing with room air. In one recently published paper, the authors reviewed seven studies where subjects were exposed to passive marijuana smoke and concluded that, when cannabinoids are detected in the urine using conventional drugs of abuse testing, such results are commensurate with active smoking of marijuana [28].

Niedlbala et al. studied the effect of passive inhalation of marijuana on urine and oral fluid testing using high marijuana containing cigarettes. In Study 1 four smokers smoked THC mixed with tobacco (39.5 mg THC) in an unventilated eight passenger van and four volunteers were exposed to marijuana smoke (passive inhalation). In Study 2 four volunteers smoked marijuana only (83.2 mg THC). Oral fluid was collected using Intercept Oral Specimen Collection Device (OraSure Technology, Bethlehem, PA). Participants were allowed to go outside the van 60 min after exposure. Oral fluid and urine specimens were collected. Oral fluids were tested for THC metabolite using a cut-off of 3 ng/mL (confirmation: 2.0 ng/mL) and for urine specimens, the cut-off was 50 ng/mL. All urine specimens tested negative (50 ng/mL cut-off) for all passive smokers (GC/MS showed THC metabolite concentration in the range 5.8–14.7 ng/mL 8 h after exposure). In Study 1 where oral fluid was collected in the van, some subjects showed positive response due to contamination of the device with THC smoke but in Study 2 when all oral fluid specimens were collected outside the van no positive specimens were observed [29].

4.2 Consumption of Hemp Products

Industrial hemp is part of a number of varieties of *Cannabis sativa* L. which is cultivated for industrial and agricultural purpose mainly for seeds and fiber. Industrial hemp is characterized by low THC and high cannabidiol content. Because cannabidiol counteracts the pharmacological action of THC, ingestion of hemp containing products should not cause euphoria. However, cultivation of hemp trees is illegal in the United States unless a special permission is obtained from the Food and Drug Administration (FDA).

Hemp seed contains little THC and washing can remove some of the THC from the seed hull. Currently, use of hemp oil is legal but use of cannabis flowers essential oil is illegal in the United States because the cannabis flower essential oil is produced from flowering buds of cannabis plant and is considered as a marijuana product. Hemp seeds represent the starting material for the manufacturing of various products including oil, lollipops, lotion, gummy treats, tea, beer, chips, cereals, pretzels, and flour. Holler et al. analyzed 79 hemp products and observed that products analyzed prior to April 2003 contain much higher amounts of THC than products analyzed after April 2003. For example, the highest amount of THC (117.5 μg/g) found in hemp products analyzed prior to April 2003 was significantly higher than the highest amount of THC (7.8 μg/g) found among all hemp products analyzed after April 2003. In addition, no THC was detected in 58% of products analyzed prior to April 2003 compared to 86% of products analyzed after April 2003. Representative THC content of some products analyzed by these authors is given in Table 7.3. The authors concluded that THC content of hemp products available commercially today are significantly less than THC content available in the past. Therefore, probability that consumption of these products would produce urine THC metabolite level greater than 15 ng/mL is significantly reduced and should not be considered as a realistic cause for a positive urine drug test [30].

As expected, earlier studies demonstrated that the urine drug test would be positive after consumption of hemp containing products. Costantino et al. in 1997 observed that after consumption of 15 mL of hemp oil, 2 urine specimens out of 18 collected from volunteers screened greater than the 100 ng/mL cut-off for THC metabolite while 7 screened positive using the cut-off of 50 ng/mL and 14 screened positive using 20 ng/mL cut-off [31]. Struempler et al. also reported in 1997 positive cannabinoid workplace drug testing following ingestion of commercially available hemp oil preparation. The first specimen testing negative was 53 h after ingestion [32]. The highest amount of THC metabolite (431 ng/mL) was reported by a Swiss research group after volunteers consumed cannabis seed oil containing 1500 μg/g of THC. In addition, urine samples were positive up to 6 days after ingestion of oil [33]. Another report from Switzerland confirmed THC poisoning in four patients after eating salad preparation containing hemp oil because the concentrations of THC in the hemp oil far exceeded the recommended tolerance dose [34]. Following this report, Swiss Federal Office of Public Health issued a warning concerning consumption of hemp oil. More recent reports from the United States indicate that drinking moderate amounts of hemp oil should not cause THC positive results in workplace drug testing. Leson et al. reported that consumption of 125 mL of hemp oil (equivalent to ingestion of 0.6 mg of THC, a very high consumption) produced highest THC metabolite concentration of 5.2 ng/mL as determined by GC/MS. This value was below the 15 ng/mL cut-off of GC/MS confirmation [35].

Table 7.3 High THC content of hemp some products analyzed before April 2003 and after April 2003

Manufacturer	Product type	Amount of THC (μg/g)	Year analyzed
Analyzed before April 21, 2003			
Spectrum essential	Oil	117.5	1998
Spectrum essential	Capsule	68.5	2002
Spectrum essential	Oil	29.5	2002
Hempola	Oil	11.5	1998
Hempsted	Oil	21.0	1998
Hempsted	Oil	12.6	2002
Health from the Sun	Capsule	18.6	1998
HempNut	Oil	90.4	2002
Analyzed after April 21, 2003			
Nutiva	Oil	7.8	2003
Nutiva	Oil	7.4	2004
Viridian	Oil	7.5	2004
Chronic candy	Lollipop	1.04	2007

Source: Holler et al. [30]. Modified from the original table

5 Case Study

The following case was taken from MRO Case Studies, a publication of SAMHSA (Health and Human Services of the US Government) [36].

Case Report: During interview the donor claimed that the positive test result of marijuana metabolite (30 ng/mL) was due to passive inhalation of marijuana at a party he attended. The donors' specimen was collected 2 days after attending the party. Clinical studies clearly indicate that it is highly unlikely to test positive for marijuana metabolite at a SAMHSA mandated cut-off concentration from passive inhalation of marijuana. The MRO reported the marijuana test as positive.

6 Conclusions

Eating poppy seed containing products may lead to positive opiate screening test results and the presence of codeine and morphine in urine can also be confirmed by using gas chromatography-mass spectrometry because poppy seed contains both morphine and codeine. The presence of 6-monoacetylmorphine in urine indicates heroin abuse and is not consistent with the consumption of poppy seed containing food. Although the presence of thebaine may confirm consumption of poppy seed containing food, its absence does not rule out ingestion of poppy seed containing product by an individual. Passive inhalation of marijuana is unlikely to lead to a positive urine test for the presence of marijuana metabolite. In addition, amounts of

THC found in hemp products today are very small and therefore consumption of hemp products is also unlikely to cause positive test result.

References

1. Schmidt J, Boettcher C, Kuhnt C, Zenk MH. Poppy alkaloid profiling by electrospray tandem mass spectrometry and electrospray FT-ICR mass spectrometry after [ring-13C]-tyramine feeding. Phytochemistry 2007; 68: 189–202.
2. Reid RG, Durham DG, Boyle SP, Low AS, Wangboonskul J. Differentiation of opium and poppy straw using capillary electrophoresis and pattern recognition techniques. Anal Chim Acta 2007; 605: 20–27.
3. Pelders M, Ross JJ. Poppy seeds: difference in morphine and codeine content and variation in inter-and intra individual excretion. J Forensic Sci 1996; 41: 209–212.
4. Hill V, Cairns T, Cheng CC, Schaffewr M. Multiple aspects of hair analysis for opiates: methodology, clinical and workplace population, codeine and poppy seed ingestion. J Anal Toxicol 2005; 29: 696–703.
5. Thevis M, Opfermann G, Schanzer W. Urinary concentrations of morphine and codeine after consumption of poppy seeds. J Anal Toxicol 2003; 27: 53–56.
6. Keskin O, Sekerel BE. Poppy seed allergy: a case report and review of literature. Allergy Asthma Proc 2006; 27: 396–398.
7. Panasoff J. Poppy seed anaphylaxis. J Investig Allergol Clin Immunol 2008; 18: 224–225.
8. Unnithan S, Strang J. Poppy tea dependance. Br J Psychiatry 1993; 163: 813–814.
9. Sttentoff A, Kaa E, Worm K. Fatal intoxication in Denmark following intake of morphine from opium poppies. Z Rechtsmed 1988; 101: 197–204.
10. King M, McDonough MA, Drummer OH, Berkovic SF. Poppy tea and the baker's first seizure. Lancet 1997; 350: 716.
11. Van Thuyne W, Van Eenoo P, Delbeke FT. Urinary concentrations of morphine after the administration of herbal tea containing Papaveris fructus in relation to doping analysis. J Chromatogr B Analyt Technol Biomed Life Sci 2003; 785: 245–251.
12. Fraser AD, Worth D. Experience with a urine opiate screening and confirmation cutoff of 2000 ng/mL. J Anal Toxicol 1999; 23: 549–551.
13. Fritschi G, Prescott WR. Morphine levels in urine subsequent to poppy seed consumption. Forensic Sci Int 1985; 27: 111–117.
14. Struempler RE. Excretion of codeine and morphine following ingestion of poppy seeds. J Anal Toxicol 1987; 11: 97–99.
15. Hayes LW, Krassolt WG, Mueggier PA. Concentrations of morphine and codeine in serum and urine after ingestion of poppy seeds. Clin Chem 1987; 33: 806–808.
16. Meadway C, George S, Braithwaite R. Opiate concentrations following the ingestion of poppy seeds products—evidence for poppy seed defense. J Forensic Sci 1998; 96: 29–38.
17. Sproll C, Perz RC, Lachenmeier DW. Optimized LC/MS analysis of morphine and codeine in poppy seed and evaluation of their fate during food processing as a basis of risk analysis. J Agric Food Chem 2006; 54: 5292–5298.
18. Lo DS, Chan TH. Poppy seeds: implications of consumption. Med Sci Law 1992; 32: 296–302.
19. Moeller MR, Hammer K, Engel O. Poppy seed consumption and toxicological analysis of blood and urine samples. Forensic Sci Int 2004; 143: 183–186.
20. Trafkowski J, Madea B, Musshoff F. The significance of putative urinary markers of illicit heroin use after consumption of poppy seed products. Ther Drug Monit 2006; 28: 552–558.
21. Rohrig TP, Moore C. The determination of morphine in urine and oral fluid following ingestion of poppy seeds. J Anal Toxicol 2003; 27: 449–452.
22. Meneely KD. Poppy seed ingestion: the Oregon experience. J Forensic Sci 1992; 37: 1158–1162.

23. Liu HC, Ho HO, Liu RH, Yeh GC, Lin DL. Urinary excretion of morphine and codeine following the administration of single and multiple doses of opium preparations prescribed in Taiwan as "brown mixture." J Anal Toxicol 2006; 30: 225–231.
24. von Euler M, Villen T, Svensson JO, Stahle L. Interpretation of the presence of 6-monoacetylmorphine in the absence of morphine-3-glucuronide in urine samples: evidence of heroin abuse. Ther Drug Monit 2003; 25: 645–648.
25. Cone EJ, Clarke J, Tsanaclis L. Prevalance and disposition of drugs of abuse and opioid treatment drugs in oral fluid. J Anal Toxicol 2007; 31: 424–433.
26. Al-Amri AM, Smith RM, El-Haj BM, Juma's MH. The GC-MS detection and characterization of reticuline as a marker for opium use. Forensic Sci Int 2004; 142: 61–69.
27. Cassella G, Wu AH, Shaw BR, Hill DW. The analysis of thebaine in urine for the detection of poppy seed consumption. J Anal Toxicol 1997; 21: 376–383.
28. Westin AA, Slordal L. Passive inhalation of cannabis smoke-is it detectable?. Tidsskr Nor Laegeforen 2009; 129: 109–113.
29. Niedbala RS, Kardos KW, Fritch D, Kunsman K, Blum KA, Newland GA et al. Passive cannabis smoke exposure and oral fluid testing II. Two studies of extreme cannabis smoke exposure in a motor vehicle. J Anal Toxicol 2005; 29: 607–615.
30. Holler JM, Bosy TZ, Dunkley CS, Levine B et al. Delta-9-tetrahydrocannabinol content of commercially available hemp products. J Anal Toxicol 2008; 32: 428–432.
31. Costantino A, Schwartz RH, Kaplan P. Hemp oil ingestion causes positive urine tests for delta-9-tetrahydrocannabinol carboxylic acid. J Anal Toxicol 1997; 21: 482–485.
32. Struempler RE, Nelson G, Urry TM. A positive cannabinoid workplace drug test following the ingestion of hemp seed oil. J Anal Toxicol 1997; 21: 283–285.
33. Lehman T, Sager F, Brenneisen R. Excretion of cannabinoids in urine after ingestion of cannabis seed oil. J Anal Toxicol 1997; 5: 373–375.
34. Meier H, Vonesch HJ. Cannabis poisoning after eating salad. Schweiz Med Wochenschr 1997; 127: 214–218.
35. Leson G, Pless P, Grotenhermen F, Kalant H, ElSohly MA. Evaluating the impact of hemp food consumption on workplace drug tests. J Anal Toxicol 2001; 25: 691–698.
36. MROCase Studies (Health and Human Services of the US Government) 2005: (http://workplace.samhsa.gov/DrugTesting/Files_Drug_Testing/MROs/MRO%20Case%20Studies%20%20Ferbruary%202005.pdf)

Chapter 8
Defending Positive Cocaine Tests

Abstract People try to defend positive cocaine test results by claiming they drink herbal tea or visit a dentist who uses procaine as an anesthetic. Although a positive cocaine test result as confirmed urinary benzoylecgonine may result from drinking coca tea, the import of such tea in the United States is illegal. Nevertheless, there are few reports in the literature describing the presence of cocaine in certain herbal teas. Procaine does not contain cocaine and use of procaine cannot result in positive test results. Although some reports describe the presence of cocaine and other drugs of abuse in paper currencies of the United States and other countries, handling such paper money cannot produce a positive drug test in the urine.

Keywords Health inca tea · Mate De Coca · Positive cocaine

1 Introduction

Cocaine is a popular drug of abuse worldwide. During the 1980s, the social distribution of adult cocaine use in the United States became more prevalent in the lower social strata compared to the upper strata [1]. In contrast, in Australia the majority of cocaine users interviewed were classified as socially and economically integrated as they were well-educated, employed young people who generally snorted cocaine on a recreational basis [2]. Cocaine has a very short half-life in blood. Therefore, in workplace drug testing, cocaine abuse is determined by confirming the presence of benzoylecgonine, a major metabolite of cocaine in the urine specimen. Cocaine is a Class II scheduled drug and is very infrequently used in medical practice as a topical anesthetic by ENT specialists. Such use of cocaine may cause positive urine test results (see Chap. 10 for more details). Popular defenses for people tested positive for cocaine are use of herbal tea and exposure to procaine.

A. Dasgupta, *Beating Drug Tests and Defending Positive Results*,
DOI 10.1007/978-1-60761-527-9_8, © Springer Science+Business Media, LLC 2010

2 Herbal Tea and Cocaine

Coca tea, also known as "Mate de Coca" and "Health Inca Tea" is a herbal tea prepared from coca leaves (*Erythroxylum coca*). Coca leaves contain cocaine but it would take about 500 g of coca leaves to prepare 1 g of cocaine. The custom of chewing coca leaves in the Andes Mountain regions of South America dates back at least to 3,000 BC. Chewing coca leaves suppresses the sensation of hunger, provides more energy during long days of work and helps to counter altitude sickness. The Incas chewed coca leaves with lime and swallowed the juice which allowed them to work long hours without eating or drinking. It was observed in the nineteenth century that coca leaves placed in wounds provided pain relief [3]. Today, millions of people chew coca in Bolivia, Colombia, Peru, Northern Argentina and Chile. In addition, chewing coca leaves has ritual, religious and cultural significance in these South American countries [4]. Because chewing coca leaves or drinking coca tea increases the absorption of oxygen in the blood and may help combat altitude sickness, on the "Inca Trail" to Machu Picchu guides usually serve coca tea with every meal so that visitors are more at ease with the high altitude. Usually government officials traveling to La Paz, Bolivia are greeted with "Mate De Coca" because the altitude of the place is 4,000 m above sea level (13,120 ft; 1 m = 3.28 ft). When Princess Anne and the late Pope John Paul II were visiting Bolivia, they were also greeted with coca tea [5]. Coca chewers do not present hypoglycemia at high altitude due to an antagonistic effect of coca metabolites on insulin, allowing a greater availability of glucose for individuals [6]. Favier et al. studied the effects of acute coca use on the hormonal and metabolic responses of non-habitual coca chewers. The authors used 12 healthy non-habitual coca users. On one occasion they were asked to chew 15 g of coca leaves 1 h before exercise and, on another occasion, exercise was performed 1 h after chewing a sugar free chewing gum. At rest, coca chewing had no effect on plasma hormonal or metabolic effect except for a significantly reduced insulin level. During exercise, the oxygen uptake, heart rate, and respiratory gas exchange ratio were significantly increased in the coca chewing trial compared with the gum chewing test. The exercise induced drop in plasma glucose level was also prevented by coca chewing [7]. In 1961, the United Nation's Single Convention of Narcotic Drugs placed coca leaves in the same category as cocaine and ordered that coca leaf chewing must be abolished within 25 years after signed at the convention. Bolivia signed the convention in 1976 and the 25 years deadline expired in 2001. Therefore, under this convention, millions of people currently chewing coca leaves to maintain the tradition are in violation of an international law [4].

South American Indians have used coca leaf as a remedy for thousands of years. Coca might be helpful for treating gastrointestinal problems and motion sickness, and is a substitute for coffee as a stimulant. Coca leaf also has an antidepressant effect and may also be used for weight reduction and improving physical fitness. In leaf form, coca does not produce dependency or toxicity and its effects are very different from cocaine [8]. Coca also regulates carbohydrate metabolism and may provide a new therapeutic approach to hypoglycemia and diabetes mellitus. With low dose chronic administration, it appears to normalize body function and again, in leaf form, coca does not produce toxicity or dependence [9].

Coca tea can be prepared by submerging coca leaves into water. Coca tea is also sold commercially in filtering tea bags containing approximately 1 g of coca leaves. Like decaffeinated coffee, cocaine can be removed from coca leaves and such tea can be sold legally in the United States [4]. However, even after removing cocaine, a residual small amount of cocaine may still remain in the coca tea. Agwa de Bolivia Coca Leaf Liqueur is another product derived from coca leaves. Coca tea where cocaine has not been removed contains a significant amount of cocaine. Although coca tea legally available in the United States market should not contain any cocaine, there are several reports in the literature describing substantial amounts of benzoylecgonine in the urine of subjects who drank such tea.

2.1 Coca Tea and Urinary Level of Benzoylecgonine

Drinking coca tea is equivalent to consumption of cocaine. Therefore, a positive cocaine test result in the urine is expected after consumption of such tea. In one study authors found an average of 5.11 mg of cocaine per tea bag of coca tea that originated from Peru and an average of 4.86 mg of cocaine per tea bag in Bolivian coca tea. When tea was prepared, one cup of Peruvian coca tea had an average of 4.14 mg of cocaine while one cup of Bolivian tea had an average of 4.29 mg of cocaine. When one volunteer drank one cup of Peruvian tea, a peak benzoylecgonine concentration of 3,940 ng/mL was observed 10 h post consumption. Similarly, consumption of one cup of Bolivian tea by a volunteer resulted in a peak benzoylecgonine concentration of 4,979 ng/mL 3.5 h after consumption of tea [10]. Jackson et al. reported urinary concentration of benzoylecgonine after ingestion of one cup of health Inca tea by volunteers. Benzoylecgonine was detected up to 26 h post ingestion. Maximum urinary benzoylecgonine concentration varied from 1,400 to 2,800 ng/mL after ingestion of health Inca tea [11]. Mazor et al. studied the effect of drinking coca tea on excretion of cocaine metabolite in urine. Five healthy volunteers consumed coca tea and underwent serial urine testing for cocaine metabolites using the fluorescence polarization immunoassay. Each participant showed positive urine sample (over 300 ng/mL cut-off for cocaine metabolite) within 2 h of drinking coca tea and urine specimens from three out of five volunteers showed positive test results for up to 36 h. Mean benzoylecgonine concentration was 1,777 ng/mL (range: 1065–2495) [12]. Turner et al. reported positive tests for cocaine metabolite in subjects after drinking Mate de Coca tea. Tea was prepared by allowing one Mate de Coca tea bag to be immersed in 250 mL boiling water for 25 min. The bag was removed and squeezed in tea to drain additional water. A 5-mL sample was taken for analysis and volunteers drank the rest. Urinary samples were collected from 2 to 68 h after drinking tea. All urine samples tested positive for benzoylecgonine. The amount of cocaine in the tea was estimated to be 2.5 mg [13]. Typical cocaine content of coca tea is summarized in Table 8.1.

Table 8.1 Cocaine content in various coca teas

Tea	Average cocaine content	Reference
Peruvian coca tea	5.11 mg/tea bag	10
Bolivian coca tea	4.86 mg/tea bag	10
Peruvian tea (one cup)	4.14 mg	10
Bolivian tea (one cup)	4.29 mg	10
Mate de coca (one cup)	2.5 mg	13

2.2 Legal Consequence of Positive Cocaine Due to Ingestion of Coca Tea

Coca leaves usually contain less than 1% cocaine but cocaine must be removed to sell such tea in the United States. But like decaffeinated coffee, residual cocaine may still be present after "de-cocainization" of coca leaves. A 2nd Class Petty Navy Officer visited San Antonio in May 2008 where he was offered a herbal tea from Mexico. He liked the tea and brought some tea back home. He later failed a drug test and he blamed the herbal tea for the positive cocaine test result. The herbal tea was identified as "Mate De Coca" and when a tea bag was tested by the National Toxicology Laboratories, Inc. in Bakersfield, CA, 4.8 mg of cocaine was found in the tea bag. The tea consumed by the person was directly bought from Windsor, the company that makes them at a cost of $15 for 100. The navy officer had to face a court-marshal and was found guilty. This was the first time this officer failed a drug test due to ingestion of coca tea [14].

However, in another case, the Illinois Court of Appeals ruled on June 9, 2004 that a woman fired from her job at the Cook County should be reinstated because she tested positive in cocaine drug testing due to drinking coca tea. She was completely unaware that coca tea may contain cocaine. The petitioner was hired by the Cook County Sheriff's Office in January 1990 and was continuously employed there as a deputy sheriff until her termination in January 2001 due to a failed drug test. On October 5, 2000, as a part of drug free workplace policy, the petitioner was randomly selected for a workplace drug testing and the Quest Diagnostic Laboratory reported that the petitioner's urine was positive for the presence of cocaine metabolites (307 ng/mL of benzoylecgonine). The petitioner's husband who was employed as a Chicago police officer testified that they went to Peru to adopt a baby. When the infant, at the time 7 months old, became sick, they took her to the American hospital in Lima, Peru where the doctor recommended "Mate De Coca" for the baby and gave them a few tea bags. The doctor assured them that cocaine was removed from the tea. They brought the tea through the United States Customs without any problem and ordered more tea through the Internet. Since then the petitioner drank the tea from time to time. After the petitioner failed the drug test, she returned to Peru and purchased additional boxes of "Mate De Coca" and photographed them as they appeared on the shelves of the local supermarkets in Peru. He also ordered more tea through the Internet to demonstrate that, although it was illegal, cocaine containing tea can be available on the United States market. Based on testimonies by the expert witness, her hair analysis results and analysis of the tea bag by a separate Toxicology Reference laboratory, the Illinois Court of Appeals reversed the decision of the Merit Board to dismiss the petitioner and also reversed the order of the Circuit Court of Cook County affirming the Merit Board's decision [15].

Because of the possibility of testing positive for cocaine following drinking coca tea, it is advisable to avoid any herbal tea originating from South America at least for few weeks prior to any workplace drug testing.

3 Mugwort and Positive Cocaine

Hickey et al. reported an interesting case where a 47-year-old female who had undergone several surgeries was managed on narcotic pain medications including opioids. The policy of the authors' hospital requires these patients to undergo periodic drug testing to ensure that they are not abusing illicit drugs. On October 31, 2001, the patient's urine screened positive for benzoylecgonine at a cut-off concentration of 300 ng/mL using the fluorescence polarization immunoassay (FPIA, Abbott Laboratories, Abbott Park, IL). The patient denied any cocaine abuse but claimed that she may have been exposed to passive inhalation of crack cocaine because her neighbor upstairs was a crack addict. A second specimen submitted by the patient on November 2, 2001 also tested positive for benzoylecgonine, but at that time the patient claimed taking mugwort, a herbal supplement. This herb is used as a bitter digestive tonic, menstrual regulator and antirheumatic. Results from gas chromatography/mass spectrometry (GC/MS) confirmed the presence of benzoylecgonine in both urine specimens. When the authors purchased mugwort from a local herbal store (which was identified by a herbalist) and prepared tea, the tea tested negative for all drugs of abuse tested. However, the mugwort sample submitted by the patient appeared darker, more finely crushed, and coated with a white granular powder while the authentic mugwort identified by the herbalist was lighter in color, contained more flowers and leaves and did not seem to have the same coating of white powder. When the authors prepared tea from the mugwort specimen submitted by the patient, it tested positive for cocaine metabolite (above linearity; >5,000 ng/mL) but tested negative for amphetamines, barbiturates, benzodiazepines, opiates, and cannabinoids. It appeared that someone may have contaminated mugwort with cocaine and cocaine metabolite [16].

4 Procaine and Workplace Drug Testing

Procaine, chemically known as 2-(diethylamino)ethyl-4-aminobenzoate is a local anesthetic used to reduce pain of intramuscular injection of penicillin and is also used in dental practice. Procaine is sold as Novocain® and has no structural similarity with cocaine. It is metabolized by the pseudocholinesterase enzyme of the human serum into para-aminobenzoic acid which is structurally very different from benzoylecgonine, the major metabolite of cocaine. Therefore defending positive cocaine results in workplace drug testing as being due to the use of procaine has no merit.

Although procaine was widely used in the past, now lidocaine has mostly replaced the use of procaine in dental practice. Prior to the discovery of procaine, cocaine was used as a local anesthetic. Procaine, like cocaine, can constrict blood vessels. This reduces bleeding but produces an anesthetic effect without the euphoria and addictive properties of cocaine. Because procaine is metabolized by the pseudo-cholinesterase, people with a deficiency of this enzyme may experience a prolonged period of high level of this anesthetic in the blood. Downham et al. reported systematic toxic reaction in 8 out of 10,469 patients during or immediately following intramuscular injection of 4,800,000 units of procaine penicillin G for the treatment of gonorrhea. The symptoms including fear of imminent death, confusion, violent combativeness, and grand mal seizure closely parallel systematic toxic reaction to a local anesthetic. The plasma pseudocholinesterase activities in patients who had experienced toxic reaction were significantly lower compared to that of controls [17].

5 Benzocaine, Tetracaine, Lidocaine, and Workplace Drug Testing

People also blame benzocaine, tetracaine, and lidocaine for positive workplace cocaine tests. Although all these drugs ends with a "caine," none of these drugs have any structural similarity with cocaine or its metabolite and thus cannot produce positive cocaine test results in a drug testing. Benzocaine is derived from aminobenzoic acid and is a useful topic anesthetic. It is used in many over-the-counter compounds for pruritus and pain and usually has a low incidence of toxicity. Lidocaine is also a local anesthetic and causes loss of feeling to the skin and the surrounding tissue. Lidocaine is also an anti-arrhythmic drug but due to poor bioavailability cannot be given orally. Chemical structure of lidocaine and cocaine is given in Fig. 8.1 to show how different is the chemical structure of lidocaine from cocaine.

Tetracaine is also a local anesthetic which is used in ophthalmologic procedures and also for other purposes. Although the use of tetracaine should not produce any positive drug test, a combination of tetracaine, adrenalin, and cocaine (TAC) has become increasingly popular as a topical anesthetic for the suturing of simple skin lacerations and application of such an anesthetic may produce positive cocaine urine drug testing results. In one study, on the morning after using TAC, 14 out of 18 patients (78%) screened positive by the EMIT immunoassay cocaine test (Syva, San Jose, CA). When all urine specimens were analyzed by gas chromatography/mass spectrometry, 15 out of 18 specimens (83%) were positive. Positive test results in the urine specimen may occur up to 48 h after the use of TAC and the authors recommended that physicians should communicate this information to their patients [18].

Fig. 8.1 Chemical structure of lidocaine and cocaine

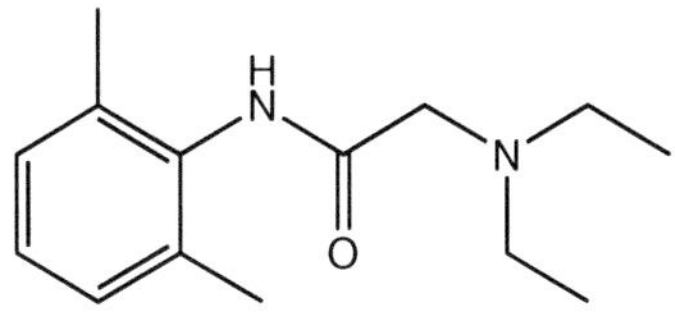

Lidocaine

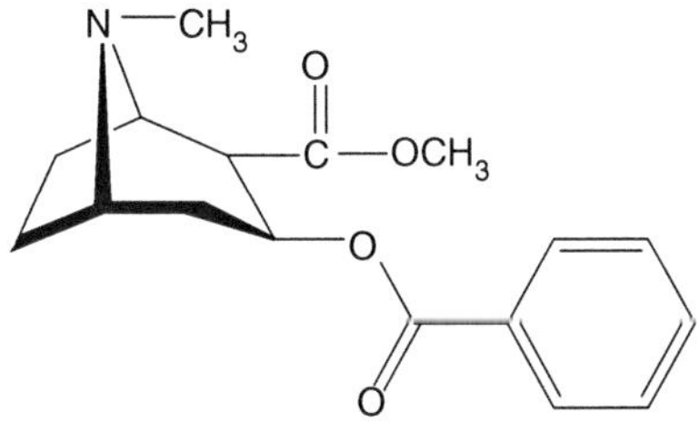

Cocaine

Sometimes street cocaine is cut with benzocaine and abuse of such a product may cause severe methemoglobinemia. A 27-year-old man ingested a large quantity of street cocaine in a suicide attempt. Shortly after that he became cyanotic and developed tonic-clonic seizure. Hemoglobin analysis demonstrated severe methemoglobinemia. Testing of cocaine revealed the presence of benzocaine [19]. Cocaine is also cut using lidocaine (rock cocaine), procaine, or tetracaine [20].

6 Paper Money Contaminated with Cocaine

Cocaine has been isolated from United States currency as well as currencies from other countries [21–25]. Oyler et al. examined $1 bills from several big cities in the United States for the presence of cocaine by extracting dollar bills using methanol. The presence of cocaine was confirmed by gas chromatography/mass spectrometry (GC/MS). The authors found cocaine in 74% of the bills in amounts above 0.1 μg. Moreover, 54% of currency showed cocaine concentration above 1.0 μg. The highest amount of cocaine found was 1,327 μg in a $1 bill [21]. Negrusz et al. analyzed ten $20 bills collected from Rockford, IL and four $1 bills collected from Chicago. The concentration of cocaine varied from 10.02 to 0.14 μg in $20 bills and 2.99 μg to none detected in $1 bills. Overall, 92.8% of all bills analyzed were contaminated with cocaine [22]. Jenkins reported the analysis of ten randomly collected US $1 bills from five cities for cocaine, 6-acetylmorphine, morphine, codeine, methamphetamine, amphetamine, and phencyclidine. Bills were immersed in acetonitrile for 2 h in order to extract these drugs followed by confirmation of these drugs using gas chromatography/mass spectrometry (GC/MS). The author observed cocaine in 92% of these dollar bills analyzed with concentrations of cocaine varying from 0.01 to 922.7 μg per bill (median: 1.4 μg per bill). In addition, 6-monoacetyl morphine (a metabolite of heroin) and morphine were detected in three bills while amphetamine was detected in one bill. The author further reported that methamphetamine was present in three bills and phencyclidine (PCP) in two bills (0.78 and

1.87 μg per bill). This report demonstrates that, although cocaine is the major contamination of US paper currency, other abused drugs may also be present [23]. Zuo et al. detected cocaine in 67% of the circulated bank-notes collected in Southern Massachusetts. The amount of cocaine varied from 2 ng to 49.4 μg per note. On average, $5, $10, $20, and $50 bills contain higher amounts of cocaine than $1 and $100 bills [24].

Lavins et al. analyzed 165 randomly collected paper currency notes from 12 US cities and 4 foreign countries and analyzed for the presence of delta-9-tetrahydrocannabinol (THC), cannabinol and cannabidiol, 11-nor-9-carboxy-delta-9-tetrahydrocannabinol, and 11-hydroxy-delta-9-tetrahydrocannabinol. Uncirculated dollar bills were used as the control. The authors reported for US $1 bills (n = 125) that THC was present in only two bills (1.6%) with concentrations 0.085 and 0.146 μg. The authors detected the presence of cannabinol in 13 dollar bills (10.31%) with a range of values between 0.014 and 0.774 μg. Cannabidiol was present in two bills with concentrations of 0.032 and 0.086 μg. For foreign currencies (n = 40) THC and cannabinol were detected in 9 notes (22.5%). These currency notes were from Colombia, India, Qatar, and New Zealand and the concentrations of THC ranged from 0.026 to 0.065 μg/bill and cannabinol concentrations ranged from 0.061 to 0.197 μg/bill [25]. There are several studies which recorded the presence of only low nanogram levels of cocaine in paper currencies. Hudson analyzed the cocaine content of all denominations obtained through the Bank of Canada in Regina and Saskatchewan and observed that the cocaine levels were typically less than 1 ng per bank-note, although some worn out and dirty notes showed the presence of higher amounts of cocaine. The authors also analyzed five groups of notes seized as a result of drug investigation and reported range of cocaine levels from 2.7 to 1,069 ng per note [26]. Typical concentrations of cocaine and other illicit drugs in United States paper currencies are given in Table 8.2.

The main reason that such a high percentage of paper currencies are contaminated with cocaine is that cocaine is present as a fine powder and when a person rolls up a bill to snort cocaine, a trace of cocaine may stick to the bill. In addition, money is also contaminated during drug deals. As money is counted in machines in banks, machines become contaminated and transfer small amounts of cocaine to subsequent bills [23].

6.1 Handling Money Contaminated with Cocaine and Drug Testing

A very small amount of cocaine is absorbed from the skin. Therefore, a very small amount of cocaine may be found in the urine after topical exposure to cocaine. A 5-mg dose of cocaine free base was applied to the forearm skin surface of a volunteer and urinary benzoylecgonine concentrations were determined. The maximum urinary concentration of benzoylecgonine of 55 ng/mL was observed at 48 h and a total of 58 μg of cocaine (1.2% of the total dose) was excreted in the 96-h urine. An

Table 8.2 Typical levels of illicit drugs found in currencies from the United States

Drug	Amount found	Reference
Cocaine	1,327 μg	20
Cocaine	2.99 μg	21
Cocainc	10.02 μg	21
Cocaine	922.7 μg	22
Cocaine	233.3 μg	22
Cocaine	49.4 μg	23
Heroin	168.5 μg	22
Morphine	5.51 μg	22
6-Acetylmorphine	9.22 μg	22
Phencyclidine	1.87 μg	22
Amphetamine	0.85 μg	22
Methamphetamine	0.60 μg	22
Tetrahydrocannabinol (THC)	0.17 μg	24
Tetrahydrocannabinol (THC)	0.77 μg	24
Tetrahydrocannabinol (THC)	0.09 μg	24

identical trial with cocaine hydrochloride resulted in a maximum urinary benzoylecgonine concentration of only 15 ng/mL at 24 h [27]. ElSohly investigated whether individuals who handled cocaine contaminated paper money would test positive by urinalysis. Two dollar bills were immersed in dry powdered cocaine and then shaken free of loose cocaine. One individual then handled the money several times during the course of the day. Analysis of urine samples collected over a period of approximately 24 h after handling the contaminated money revealed that the maximum concentration of benzoylecgonine observed was 72 ng/mL. This value was significantly below the cut-off level of benzoylecgonine screening assay (300 ng/mL) [28]. Based on these publications, and taking into consideration the microgram quantities of cocaine or other abused drugs present in currencies, it is extremely unlikely that handling paper money contaminated with drugs would produce a positive test result in a workplace drug testing.

7 Passive Inhalation/Exposure of Cocaine

Passive inhalation of cocaine is often used as an excuse for positive workplace drug testing for cocaine. In one study, the investigators studied urinary excretion of benzoylecgonine in six male volunteers who were exposed to vapor of 100 and 200 mg freebase cocaine heated to a temperature of 200 °C in an unventilated room (12,600 L volume) for 1 h. No pharmacological effect of cocaine was detected in any subject. Urine specimens analyzed by GC/MS showed peak benzoylecgonine level between 22 and 123 ng/mL. It as estimated that the subjects on average inhaled 0.25 mg cocaine. The peak excretion time after passive inhalation was 5 h. In a second passive exposure study, research staff remained in close vicinity where the crack smokers smoked three dosages of crack (freebase) cocaine (12.5, 25, and 50 mg) over a period of 4 h. The maximum amount of cocaine detected in the urine specimen was 6 ng/mL. These results demonstrated that individuals exposed to cocaine smoke under naturalistic or artificial conditions absorbed small amounts of cocaine that were insufficient to produce positive urine specimens at the standard cut-off concentration. Only a passive exposure condition allowing absorption of cocaine in an amount of 1 mg or more could produce a positive result [29].

Crime lab personnel are often exposed to large amounts of cocaine. Le et al. reported that one criminalist who was working on a routine case of 2 kg of cocaine hydrochloride in the Narcotics Laboratory over a period of 3 h, showed a maximum urinary benzoylecgonine level of 1,570 ng/mL, which was significantly above the cut-off concentration of workplace drug testing [30]. Therefore, handling of cocaine can result in passive exposure as established by the presence of benzoylecgonine in the urine. Therefore, reducing occupational exposure to cocaine is recommended and it may reduce such exposure [31].

8 Case Studies

The following cases were taken from MRO Case Studies, a publication of SAMHSA (Health and Human Services of the US Government) [32].

Case 1: During the interview with MRO, the donor denied any cocaine use but informed that cocaine was used as a topical anesthetic during an endoscopic procedure. The donor submitted a copy of the medical record and the MRO also verified the procedure and use of cocaine by the physician. However, the procedure was performed 10 days prior to collection of the urine specimen and the detection window for detecting benzoylecgonine in urine after the topical use of cocaine is 2–3 days. Therefore, the MRO reported to the agency that the test for cocaine was positive.

Case 2: The laboratory reported urinary benzoylecgonine level of 420 ng/mL and marijuana metabolite level of 60 ng/mL. During the interview, the donor claimed that he attended a party where he ate brownies that contained marijuana and he was positive for cocaine because a dentist used lidocaine during a procedure. Although, ingestion of marijuana containing food is a popular defense, it is unlikely that the amount of marijuana present would cause a positive marijuana test result with a marijuana metabolite concentration above the cut-off. In addition, lidocaine is structurally different from cocaine (Fig. 8.1) and is not metabolized to benzoylecgonine. The MRO reported the test as positive for marijuana and cocaine.

9 Conclusions

People use various excuses to defend positive cocaine tests but other than unknowingly drinking a herbal tea prepared from coca leaves, none of the other defenses have any merit. Moreover, unknowingly drinking coca tea as the cause of positive cocaine results is only possible with a very low urinary benzoylecgonine level close to the cut-off value of 300 ng/mL which is used in the screening assay to determine the presence of benzoylecgonine in the urine. Nevertheless, the success of this defense depends on other circumstances and the judiciary, because a navy officer was found guilty by a court-marshal for a positive cocaine urine drug test due to ingestion of coca tea. It is advisable not to drink any herbal tea originating from South American countries at least for a few weeks prior to any drug test. For individuals working in more security sensitive positions where unannounced drug testing is often conducted, it will be better to avoid any such herbal tea.

Other excuses for positive cocaine test such as the dentist injected procaine or the person was exposed to other local anesthetics such as benzocaine, lidocaine, or tetracaine has no merit because none of these agents has any structural similarity with cocaine or its major metabolite benzoylecgonine. However, if a combination of tetracaine, adrenalin, and cocaine (TAC) is used, a patient may show positive urinary test for cocaine (as benzoylecgonine) for up to 48 h.

Paper currencies of the United States and other countries may be contaminated with cocaine or other drugs of abuse. However, the amount of drug present in the paper currencies are at most in microgram quantities and handling such paper money should not produce a positive workplace drug testing because only a minor fraction of cocaine is absorbed through the skin.

References

1. Miech RA, Chilcoat H, Harder VS. The increase in the association of education and cocaine use over the 1980s and 1990s: evidence for a historical period effect. Drug Alcohol Depend 2005; 79: 311–320.
2. Shearer J, Johnston J, Fry CL, Kaye S et al. Contemporary cocaine use patterns and associated harms in Melbourne and Sydney, Australia. Drug Alcohol Rev 2007; 26: 537–543.
3. Fairley HB. Anesthesia in the Inca empire. Rev Esp Anestesiol Reanim 2007; 54: 556–562.
4. Evo Morales Ayma, The President of Bolivia; New York Times opinion editorial, March 14, 2009.
5. http://en.wikipedia.org/wiki/Coca_tea Accessed 3/12/2009.
6. Galarza-Guzman M, Penaloza-Imana R, Afcha L, Aguilar Valerio M et al. Effect of coca chewing on the glucose tolerance test. Medicine (B Aries) 1997; 57: 261–264.
7. Favier R, Caceres E, Guillon L, Sempore B et al. Coca chewing for exercise: hormonal and metabolic responses of non habitual chewers. J Appl Physiol 1996; 81: 1901–1907.
8. Weil AT. Coca leaf as a therapeutic agent. Am J Drug Alcohol Abuse 1987; 5: 75–86.
9. Weil AT. The therapeutic value of coca in contemporary medicine. J Ethnopharmacol 1981; 3: 367–376.
10. Jenkins AJ, Llosa T, Montoya I, Cone EJ. Identification and quantitation of alkaloids in coca tea. Forensic Sci Int 1996; 77: 179–189.
11. Jackson GF, Saady JJ, Poklis A. Urinary excretion of benzoylecgonine following ingestion of health Inca tea. Forensic Sci Int 1991; 49: 57–64.
12. Mazor SS, Mycyk MB, Wills BK, Brace LD, Gussow L, Erickson T. Coca tea consumption causes positive urine cocaine assay. Eur J Emerg Med 2006; 13: 340–341.
13. Turner M, McCrory P. Time for tea anyone? Johnston A. Br J Sports Med 2005; 39: e37.
14. The Florida Times Union; Story by Timothy J. Gibbons; January 10, 2009; http://www.tullylegal.com, accessed 3/13/2009.
15. Garrido vs Cook County Sheriff's Merit Board, June 9, 2004, State of Illinois No-1-03–1128.

16. Hickey K, Seliem R, Shields J, McKee A et al. A positive drug test in the pain management patient: deception or herbal cross-reactivity?. Clin Chem 2002; 48: 958–960.
17. Downham TF 2nd, Cawley RA, Salley SO, Dal Santo G. Systematic toxic reaction to procaine penicillin G. Sex Transm Dis 1978; 5: 4–9.
18. Alteri M, Bogema S, Schwartz RH. TAC topical anesthesia produces positive urine test for cocaine. Ann Emerg Med 1990; 19: 577–579.
19. McKinney CD, Postiglione KF, Herold DA. Benzocaine adulterated street cocaine in association with methemoglobinemia. Clin Chem 1992; 38: 596–597.
20. Arufe-Martinez MI, Romero-Palanco JL. Identification of cocaine–lidocaine mixtures (rock cocaine) and other illicit cocaine preparations using derivative absorption spectroscopy. J Anal Toxicol 1988; 12: 192–196.
21. Oyler J, Darwin WD, Cone EJ. Cocaine contamination of United States paper currency. J Anal Toxicol 1996; 20: 213–216.
22. Negrusz A, Perry JL, Moore C. Detection of cocaine on various denominations of United States currency. J Forensic Sci 1998; 43: 626–629.
23. Jenkins AJ. Drug contamination in US paper currency. Forensic Sci Int 2001; 121: 189–193.
24. Zuo Y, Zhang K, Wu J, Rego C et al. An accurate and nondestructive GC method for determination of cocaine on US paper currency. J Sep Sci 2008; 31: 2440–2450.
25. Lavins ES, Lavins BD, Jenkins AJ. Cannabis (marijuana) contamination of United States and foreign paper currency. THC in J Anal Toxicol 2004; 28: 439–442.
26. Hudson JC. Analyses of currency of cocaine contamination. J Can Soc Forensic Sci 1989; 22: 203–219.
27. Baselt RC, Chang JY, Yoshikawa DM. On the dermal absorption of cocaine. J Anal Toxicol 1990; 14: 383–384.
28. ElSohly MA. Urinalysis and casual handling of marijuana and cocaine. J Anal Toxicol 1991; 14: 46.
29. Cone EJ, Yousefnejad D, Hillsgrove MJ, Holicky B et al. Passive inhalation of cocaine. J Anal Toxicol 1995; 19: 399–411.
30. Le SD, Taylor RW, Vidal D, Lovas JJ et al. Occupational exposure to cocaine involving crime lab personnel. J Forensic Sci 1992; 37: 959–968.
31. Gehlhausen JM, Klette KL, Stout PR, Given J. Occupational cocaine exposure of a crime laboratory personnel preparing training aids for a military working dog program. J Anal Toxicol 2003; 27: 453–458.
32. MRO Case Studies (Health and Human Services of the US Government) 2005: (http://workplace.samhsa.gov/DrugTesting/Files_Drug_Testing/MROs/MRO%20Case%20Studies%20-%20Ferbruary%202005.pdf)

Chapter 9
Defending Positive Amphetamine Results

Abstract People try to defend positive amphetamine test results by claiming the use of over-the-counter (OTC) cold medications, Vicks® inhaler, or herbal diet loss products. Although ephedrine, pseudoephedrine, and other sympathomimetic amines present in various OTC cold medications interfere with amphetamine screening assays, the gas chromatography/mass spectrometric (GC/MS) confirmatory test can easily distinguish such sympathomimetic amines from amphetamine or methamphetamine. Vicks® inhaler contains L-amphetamine which has little cross-reactivity with D-methamphetamine which is abused. Therefore, possibility of a false positive from using Vicks® inhaler in an immunoassay screening test is modest, but L-methamphetamine can be easily differentiated from D-methamphetamine by using chiral derivatization and GC/MS analysis. Although certain Chinese weight loss products may contain ephedra which may cause false positive tests in the immunoassay screening test, the GC/MS confirmation step should be negative. Therefore, none of these defenses is effective in defending positive amphetamine test results in workplace drug testing.

Keywords Cold medications · Positive amphetamine · Vicks® inhaler

1 Introduction

Amphetamine and methamphetamine, along with the designer drugs 3,4-metheyledioxy-amphetamine (MDA) and 3,4-methelenedioxymethamphetamine (Ecstasy, MDAM), are abused worldwide. These drugs are more commonly abused by adolescents and young individuals. Adolescent methamphetamine use is common and it is estimated that 5–10% of youth have used methamphetamine. Methamphetamine abuse is also associated with recent risky sexual behavior as well as adolescent pregnancy. Prevention strategies for high school students should integrate education on substance abuse, pregnancy, sexually transmitted infections, and human immunodeficiency virus [1]. In one survey using 11,375 gay and bisexual men in Hollywood and West Hollywood, California, the authors

A. Dasgupta, *Beating Drug Tests and Defending Positive Results*,
DOI 10.1007/978-1-60761-527-9_9,

reported that between January and June 1999, 46.0% of subjects reported recent methamphetamine use, but a survey between July and December 2007 revealed that only 24.8% of individuals recently abused methamphetamine [2]. Ecstasy is used by adolescents who also use other illicit drugs in a poly-drug abuse pattern. There was no association between ecstasy abuse and parental social class or residential area of town. However, abuse of ecstasy was more common in house parties [3].

For workplace drug testing of amphetamines, immunoassays screening tests have antibodies either targeted to methamphetamine or amphetamine. These assays have various cross-reactivities with MDA or MDMA but there are specific immunoassays to detect the presence of ecstasy in the urine specimen.

People try to defend positive amphetamine test results by claiming taking cold medications containing pseudoephedrine, using Vicks® inhaler, or taking herbal weight loss products containing ephedra.

2 OTC and Prescription Drugs that Produce False Positives with Amphetamine/Methamphetamine Immunoassays

There are numerous OTC (over-the-counter) cold medications and other prescription medications which cross-react with various amphetamine/methamphetamine screening assays producing false positive results. Prescription and OTC medications (or metabolites of these medications) reported to interfere with amphetamines immunoassays include buflomedil, brompheniramine, chloroquine, chlorpromazine, ephedrine, fenfluramine, isometheptene, isoxsuprine, labetalol, mephentermine, mexiletine, *N*-acetylprocainamide, nylidrin, perazine, phenmetrazine, phentermine, phenylpropanolamine, promethazine, propylhexedrine, pseudoephedrine, quinacrine, ranitidine, ritodrine, tolmetin, trimethobenzamide, and tyramine [4–16].

The most commonly encountered cause of false positive results with amphetamines immunoassays is cross-reactivity with α-hydroxy amine compounds and other sympathomimetic amines found in many OTC drugs. Many false positive tests obtained by amphetamine immunoassay can be resolved by doing an alternative screening test using thin layer chromatography (TLC). Toxi-Lab is a commercially available ready to use thin layer chromatographic system available from Varian Corporation (Palo Alto, CA) for drugs of abuse testing. The process involves extraction of basic or neutral drugs from the urine specimen using prepacked extraction solvent, concentrating the organic extract, inoculation on the TLC plate, development and detection of drugs by using various developing solvents, and comparing color as well as the retention time with standards. This process can distinguish ephedrine or pseudoephedrine from amphetamine/methamphetamine, but the process is manual and may take up to 50 min. In addition, technologists performing the test and identifying drugs by visual inspections may require extensive training. The screening of amphetamine and methamphetamine using Toxi-Lab TLC system and GC/MS has been described in the literature [17].

The pretreatment of samples with sodium periodate in a basic solution eliminates interference from ephedrine, pseudoephedrine, and phenylpropanolamine by oxidative cleavage of the hydroxyl group and this reaction has been utilized in the EMIT® amphetamine confirmation kit (Dade Behring, San Jose, CA). Another strategy for elimination of false positive results is the addition of antibody to the target analyte resulting in neutralization of the signal in a true-positive sample but having no effect on the signal from a sample containing high concentrations of cross-reactive substances. In this situation, true positives are distinguished from false positives by the difference in signal before and after addition of the neutralizing antibody. This method was applied to a dual-channel neutralization procedure for amphetamines and used as a secondary screen that was effective in reducing false positives [18]. In addition, Woodworth et al. described a procedure utilizing serial dilution testing to distinguish amphetamine or methamphetamine-containing samples from samples containing cross-reacting sympathomimetic amines. Samples diluted 1:1, 1:10, and 1:20 were analyzed and maximum slope estimates (maximum change in rate over the fractional change in concentration) were determined for each compound using the EMIT® II amphetamine/methamphetamine immunoassay. The authors were able to increase the positive predictive value of the immunoassay using optimal slope cut-offs (determined by ROC analysis) to differentiate samples containing amphetamine/methamphetamine from those containing cross-reacting compounds [19]. Not all immunoassays for amphetamine/methamphetamine screening react with all the substances listed above. For example, promethazine metabolite – not the parent compound – interferes with certain amphetamine/methamphetamine immunoassays. Although individuals taking promethazine tested positive for amphetamine using the EMIT II Plus monoclonal amphetamine/methamphetamine immunoassay, no promethazine interference was observed using EMIT II Plus, Triage and TestTcard amphetamine assays or Triage methamphetamine assay [20].

Although many compounds cross-react with immunoassays for amphetamine/methamphetamine, these compounds have certain structural differences from both amphetamine and methamphetamine and should not cause false positive test result in the GC/MS confirmation step. Therefore, taking cold medication as a cause of positive amphetamine/methamphetamine test result is not an effective defense. Chemical structures of common sympathomimetic amines are given in Fig. 9.1.

3 Use of Vicks® Inhaler and Positive Methamphetamine Test

Vicks® inhaler contains L-methamphetamine, but it is D-methamphetamine which is abused. Using Vicks® inhaler is not against the law and people blame using excessive Vicks® inhaler as the cause of positive methamphetamine in the workplace drug testing. In one published report where the author re-analyzed positive amphetamine/methamphetamine urine samples by preparing chiral of (*S*)-*N*-(trifluoroacetyl)propyl derivatives, there was no instance where pure L-methamphetamine was detected in any specimen, indicating that false positive

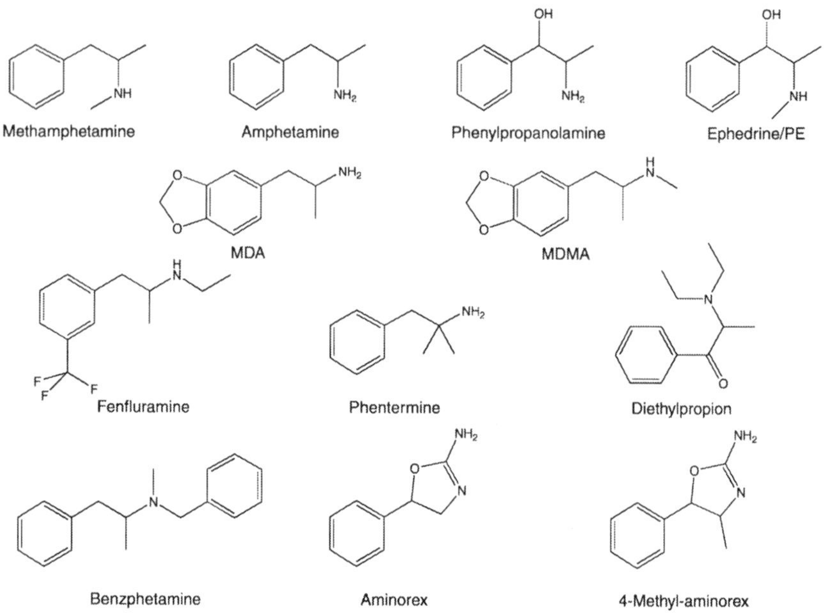

Fig. 9.1 Structures of sympathomimetic amines. Reprinted with permission from Moore KA [40] © American Association for Clinical Chemistry, Inc

methamphetamine workplace drug testing due to inhalation of L-methamphetamine is rare [21]. The reason is that L-methamphetamine has low cross-reactivity with amphetamine/methamphetamine immunoassays and are designed to detect the D isomer. Poklis et al. tested the response of EMIT II amphetamine/methamphetamine assay to specimens collected following use of Vicks® inhaler using six males and one female volunteer. Four subjects used the inhaler every two waking hours for five consecutive days while three volunteers inhaled hourly for three consecutive days. All urine voids (totaling 150 specimens) were analyzed using the EMIT II assay but none of the specimens showed any positive response at a 1,000 ng/mL cut-off of D-methamphetamine calibrator. The highest concentrations of L-methamphetamine were observed in two subjects inhaling hourly and the values were 1,390, 1,290, and 740 ng/mL respectively. These specimens were collected on the evening of the second and the third day of use. The authors concluded that, when used as directed or even double the recommended dosage, Vicks® inhaler did not produce any false positive test results with the EMIT II assay [22]. Similarly, using 1,000 ng/mL cut-off, the fluorescence polarization immunoassay for amphetamine/methamphetamine (TDxAdx/Flx assay, Abbott Laboratories, Abbott Park, IL) is unlikely to cause any false positives after recommended use of Vicks® inhaler although, when using a lower cut-off of 300 ng/mL, positive responses may occur in the immunoassay screening tests. The SAMHSA proposes to reduce the cut-off of amphetamine/methamphetamine screen to 500 ng/mL in 2010. In this event, false positive results may occur after the higher end of recommended use of Vicks® inhaler. However, in workplace drug testing, chiral derivatization followed by GC/MS analysis can resolve that issue.

Conventional GC/MS derivatization using [23] non-chiral derivatizing agents cannot resolve optical isomers. Some of the chiral derivatizing agents include *N*-trifluoroacetyl-L-propyl chloride ((S)-TPC), *R*(−)-α-methoxy-α-trifluoromethyl-phenylacetic acid chloride (MTPAC), and (−)-menthyl chloroformate. The generally accepted interpretation of isomer resolution results is that greater than 80% of the L isomer is considered consistent with use of legitimate medication or conversely greater than 20% of the D isomer (and total concentration above the cut-off) is considered evidence of illicit use.

Case Report: The laboratory confirmed the presence of methamphetamine (950 ng/mL) and amphetamine (245 ng/mL) in the urine specimen. The person tested positive denied use of any prescription medication but informed the medical review officer (MRO) regarding use of Vicks® inhaler. The MRO requested the laboratory to perform chiral analysis and the results showed that 90% of both amphetamine and methamphetamine in the specimen were D isomers. Because Vicks® inhaler contains only L-methamphetamine, the MRO reported the result as positive for methamphetamine [24].

4 Herbal Weight Loss Products and Amphetamine Assay

Although banned, some herbal weight loss products may still contain ephedra alkaloids isolated from the ephedra plant. Ephedrine is the predominant alkaloid of ephedra plants. Other phenylalanine derived alkaloids found are pseudoephedrine, norephedrine, norpseudoephedrine, *N*-methylephedrine, and phenylpropanolamine. Ephedrine is a potent central nervous system (CNS) stimulant. Because ephedra is both an α and β adrenergic agonist, ingestion of a quantity over 50 mg leads to rises in blood pressure, heart rate and cardiac output. Phenylpropanolamine is associated with cardiac toxicity. Claims have been made that ma huang is useful for the treatment of bronchial asthma, colds, flu, fever and chills, headache, and edema. Ma huang contains approximately 1% ephedrine, which has a potential to stimulate the central nervous system. Ma huang (Ephedra) is commonly found in herbal weight loss products that are often referred as to herbal fen-phen. Some weight loss clinics and herbal outlets promote "Herbal fen-phen" as an alternative to fenfluramine, the prescription drug that has been withdrawn from the market due to toxicity. Herbal fen-phen products sometimes contain St John's wort and are sold as "herbal proza." Ephedra containing products are also marketed as decongestants, bronchodilators, and stimulants. Other promoted purposes include bodybuilding and enhancement of athletic performance. "Herbal-ecstasy" is also an ephedrine-containing product which can induce a euphoric state. The FDA has strongly advised consumers not to use ephedrine containing products marketed as alternatives to street drugs.

Ma huang is dangerous in patients who have a heart condition, hypertension, diabetes, or thyroid disease, and those who are taking monoamine oxidase inhibitors. Haller and Benowitz evaluated 140 reports of ephedra related toxicity that were submitted to the FDA between June 1997 and March 31, 1999. The authors conclude that 31% of cases were definitely related to ephedra toxicity and another 31% were possibly related. As many as 47% of reports of ephedra toxicity involved cardiovascular problems and 18% involved problems with the central nervous system. Hypertension was the single most frequent adverse reaction followed by palpitation, tachycardia, stroke, and seizure. Ten events resulted in death and 13 events caused permanent disability. The authors conclude that use of a dietary supplement that contains ephedra may pose a health risk [25].

Although use of ephedra containing herbal weight loss products may cause false positive results in the amphetamine/methamphetamine screening assay, GC/MS analysis would be negative because no amphetamine or methamphetamine is naturally present in ma huang. However, there is a report of a herbal weight loss product contaminated with amphetamine derivative. A 25-year-old woman presented with abdominal pain after taking an imported herbal weight loss product. Her urine drug screen was positive for amphetamine but she denied use of any amphetamine. The analysis of the weight loss product revealed the presence of an amphetamine derivative banned by the United States Food and Drug Administration (FDA) [26].

5 Bitter Orange and Amphetamine Immunoassay

Bitter orange or Seville orange has been used in traditional Chinese medicine, and today it is used mainly as a weight loss product and also as a nasal decongestant. It is used in treating indigestion and nausea. Topically, bitter orange is used for treating ringworm and athlete's foot. Following withdrawal of ephedrine from the marketplace of dietary supplements, weight loss products containing bitter orange are gaining popularity. At this point, there is a little evidence that bitter orange may promote weight loss. However, synephrine and other structurally related compounds are present in the bitter orange, and these compounds are structurally similar to ephedra. Ingestion of these herbal supplements may increase blood pressure and heart rate. Health Canada reported that from January 1, 1998 to February 28, 2004, it received 16 reports in which products containing bitter orange or synephrine were suspected of being associated with cardiovascular adverse effects such as blackout, transient collapse, cardiac arrest, tachycardia, and ventricular fibrillation [27].

Because synephrine has some structural similarity with amphetamine, it has been hypothesized that taking bitter orange may cause false positive test results with urinary amphetamine/methamphetamine screens. In one study, six healthy adult male volunteers were administered a single dose of Nature's Way bitter orange, a 900-mg dietary supplement extract standardized to 6% synephrine. Urine specimens were collected at baseline and then at regular time intervals after the single dose of bitter orange, but none of the urine specimens tested positive by the CEDIA amphetamine assay [28].

6 False Positive GC/MS Methamphetamine Due to Ephedrine or Pseudoephedrine

In 1993, Hornbeck et al. [29] demonstrated that methamphetamine can be generated as an artifact peak in the GC/MS analysis from high levels of pseudoephedrine or ephedrine (if present in the urine specimen) in injection ports at a temperature of 300°C or above after derivatization with 4-carboethoxyhexafluorobutyryl chloride, heptafluorobutyric anhydride, and *N*-trifluoroacetyl-L-propyl chloride.. The authors investigated the effect of changing conditions and concluded that the most important conditions for this thermal conversion are the high injector temperature and high concentrations of pseudoephedrine or ephedrine. In their experiments the highest amphetamine concentration obtained was less than 50 ng/mL. Occurrence of false positive results in the federal drug testing program because of generation of methamphetamine resulted in the implementation of a requirement that, in order to report a positive methamphetamine, the metabolite amphetamine must be present at a concentration of 200 ng/mL or higher. Recommendations to prevent generation of methamphetamine include lowering the injector temperature to 185°C and also periodate pretreatment of samples. ElSohly et al. [30] showed that periodate treatment eliminated formation of methamphetamine even at the very high concentration of 1,000,000 ng/mL of pseudoephedrine, ephedrine, phenylpropanolamine, and norpseudoephedrine, because periodate selectively oxidized these compounds in the presence of amphetamine and methamphetamine. The authors used 0.35 M sodium periodate for 10 min at room temperature [30].

In addition to this artifact problem, electron impact mass spectra of trifluoroacetyl, pentafluoropropyl, heptafluorobutyl, 4-carbethoxyhexafluorobutyryl, and carbamate (prepared by derivatization with propyl chloroformate) derivatives of methamphetamine are similar to the corresponding derivatized ephedrine/pseudoephedrine. Because ephedrine and pseudoephedrine are eluted just after the methamphetamine peak, if the mass spectral analysis is not done carefully ephedrine/pseudoephedrine can be misidentified as methamphetamine. Because both ephedrine and pseudoephedrine are legal drugs and are found in over-the-counter medications, misidentification of ephedrine/pseudoephedrine as methamphetamine has a serious medical and legal implication. The chemical ionization mass spectrum of derivatized methamphetamine is very different from the derivatized ephedrine/pseudoephedrine and misidentification problem can be completely eliminated [31]. In the electron ionization mode, molecular ions of derivatized amphetamine are usually present as a very weak peak. In contrast, protonated molecular ions are the base peak (100% abundance) in the chemical ionization mass spectra of derivatized amphetamine and methamphetamine. The major mass spectral fragmentation pattern differences are given in Table 9.1. For example, in the electron ionization mode, both methamphetamine propyl carbamate and ephedrine propyl carbamate showed almost identical mass spectral fragmentation patterns (Fig. 9.2). Again, using chemical ionization where methamphetamine propyl carbamate showed a base peak at m/z 236 can circumvent this problem and the ephedrine propyl carbamate showed a base peak at m/z 192 (Fig. 9.3). The carbamate

Table 9.1 Electron ionization and chemical ionization mass spectral features of derivatized amphetamine and methamphetamine

Compound	Electron impact (m/z)	Chemical ionization (m/z)
Methamphetamine	Base: 144	Base: 236 $(M+1)^+$
Propyl carbamate	Other peaks: 102, 91, 58	Other peaks: 176, 144, 119, 58
Ephedrine propyl	Base: 144	Base: 192
Carbamate	Other peaks: 102, 77, 58	Other peaks: 220, 148, 58
Methamphetamine	Base: 154	Base: 246 $(M+1)^+$
Trifluoroacetyl	Other peaks: 118, 58	Other peaks: 154, 119
Ephedrine	Base: 154	Base: 244
Trifluoroacetyl	Other peaks: 118, 58	Other peaks: 276, 158
Methamphetamine	Base: 315	Base: 400 $(M+1)^+$
4-Carbethoxy	Other peaks: 118, 91	Other peaks: 308, 119
Ephedrine	Base: 308	Base: 398
4-Carboxy	Other peaks: 118, 91	Other peaks: 121

derivative of amphetamines can be easily prepared by adding propyl chloroformate in the organic phase containing extracted amphetamines and allowing the mixture to stand at room temperature for 10 min [31].

7 False Positive Amphetamine Due to Prescription Drug Mebeverine

Mebeverine is the veratric acid ester of a substituted ethylamphetamine derivative. This drug is used in the treatment of irritable bowel syndrome and the maximum daily prescribed dose is 200–450 mg. This drug is metabolized to mebeverine alcohol (MB–OH) and veratric acid. This process can occur in vivo and in vitro due to hydrolysis of ester bond and the parent drug is rarely detected in serum or urine of a patient receiving mebeverine. Based on rat liver microsome and human study it was postulated that MB-OH undergoes further metabolism and produces eight different compounds including amphetamine derivatives, *p*-methoxyamphetamine (PMA), and *p*-methoxyethyl-amphetamine (PMEA). The last two metabolites are also well recognized designer drugs. Elliott and Burgers presented three cases where positive amphetamine screen was due to the use of mebeverine. A 44-year-old female was found dead at home. She had been prescribed mebeverine. Citalopram (3.72 mg/L) and ethanol (209 mg/dL) were found in postmortem blood. Concentration of mebeverine was 1.2 mg/L, MB–OH 74.0 mg/L, and veratric acid 127.0 mg/L. A 32-year-old year female was found dead at home. She had been prescribed mebeverine. Her postmortem blood did not show the presence of any mebeverine but the concentrations of MB–OH and veratric acid was 6.9 and 13.7 mg/L respectively. A third case where a 20-year-old woman collapsed at home and later died at the hospital showed an anti-mortem serum levels of MB–OH and veratric acid as 5.4 and 41.8 mg/L respectively and a postmortem level MB–OH of 0.8 mg/L and veratric acid of 4.8 mg/L. Alcohol, nortriptyline,

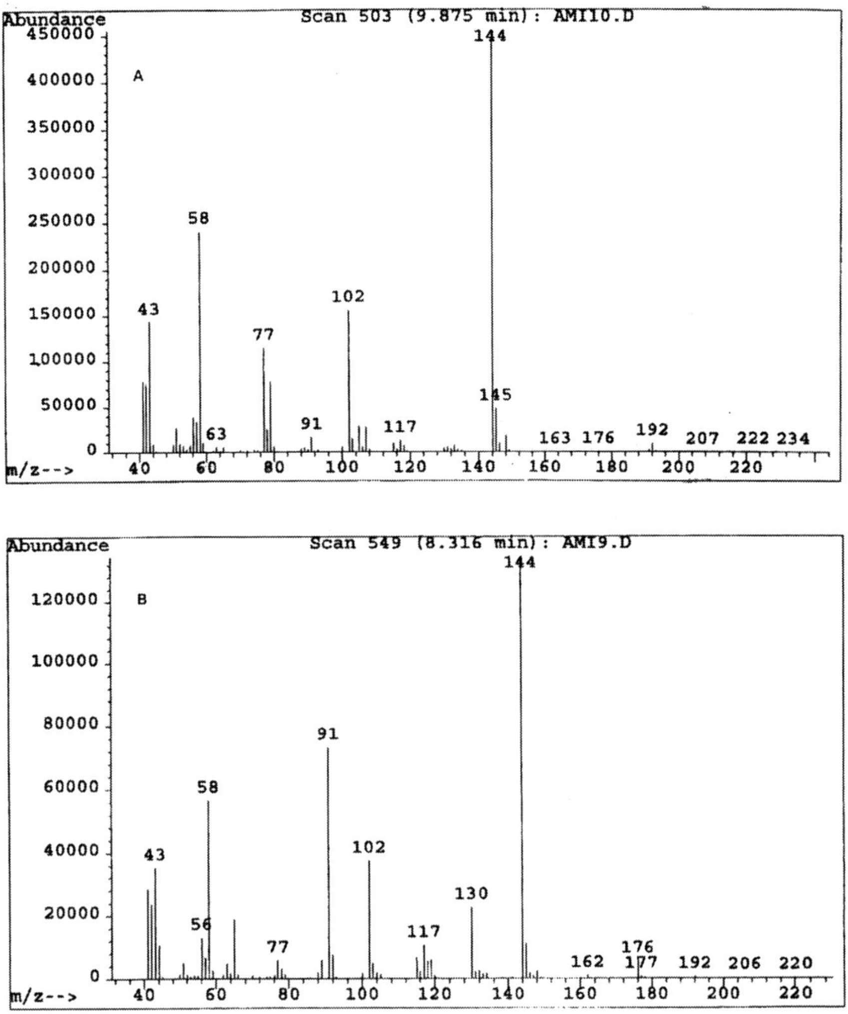

Fig. 9.2 Electron ionization mode total scan mass spectrum of (**a**) methamphetamine propyl carbamate and (**b**) ephedrine propyl carbamate (author's own data)

and carbamazepine were also found in her blood. All three patients showed positive results for amphetamine screen but the presence of PMA, PEMA, amphetamine, MDMA, and phenyl-2-ethylamine could not be confirmed by GC/MS. It is postulated that MB–OH concentration above 4.5 mg/L produced a positive response of CEDIA amphetamine assay (1,000 ng/mL cut-off) and mebeverine concentration at 6 mg/L can produce the same response. Veratric acid does not cross-react with the amphetamine assay [32]. Kraemer et al. studied the effect of mebeverine metabolite

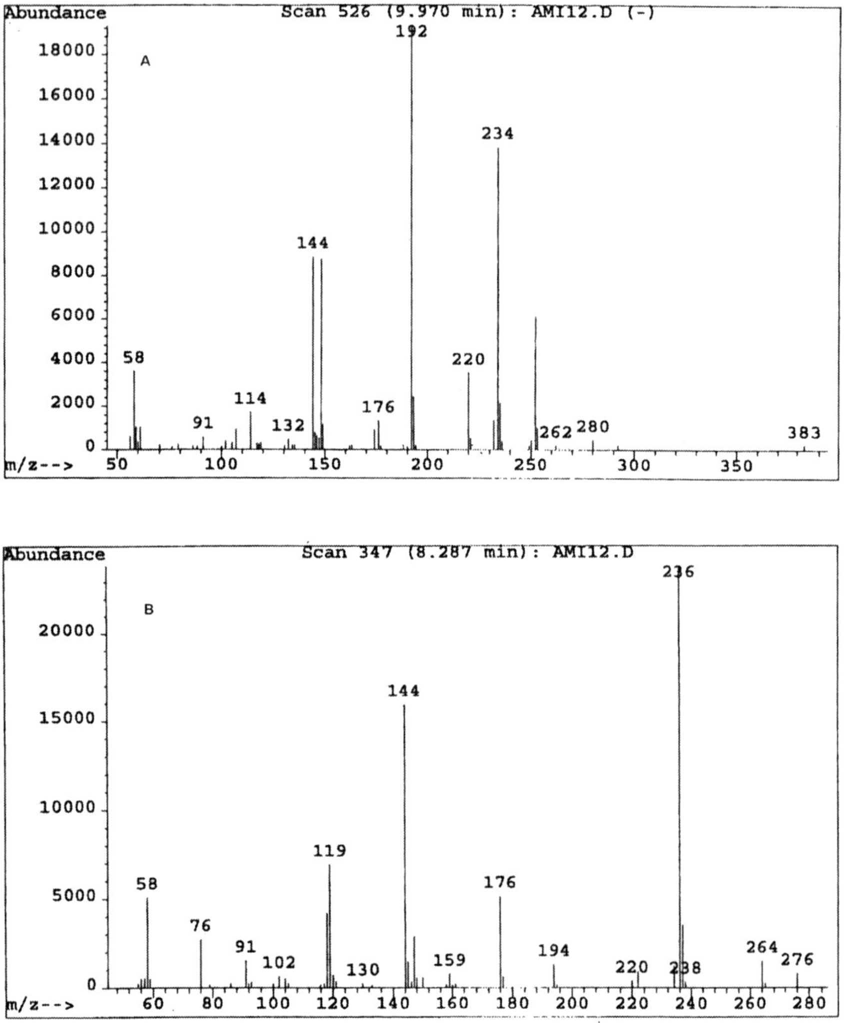

Fig. 9.3 Chemical ionization mode total ion mass spectrum of (**a**) methamphetamine propyl carbamate and (**b**) ephedrine propyl carbamate (author's own data)

on amphetamine assay and concluded that the intake of mebeverine (405 mg) leads to positive amphetamine screen by FPIA due to its metabolites methoxyethylamphetamine, hydroxyethylamphetamine, and PMA [33]. The presence of mebeverine metabolites along with the designer drugs derived from the mebeverine may explain positive amphetamine results in the workplace drug testing but unfortunately ingestion of mebeverine along with these designer drugs may also be the cause of such results.

8 Analytical True Positive Amphetamine/Methamphetamine

There are several prescription medications which contain amphetamine or methamphetamine and use of such drugs would cause positive amphetamine or methamphetamine confirmation in a workplace drug testing. In addition, several prescription medications are also metabolized to amphetamine or methamphetamine and may explain positive amphetamine drug testing results.

Amphetamine and methamphetamine are listed as Schedule II drugs in the United States and are sometimes used for treating attention deficit disorder. These drugs contain D-amphetamine, D-methamphetamine, or a racemic mixture of D and L isomers. For example, Adderall contains a mixed amphetamine salt which is used as a psychostimulant medication for treating attention deficit hyperactive disorder (ADHD). The use of Adderall is an acceptable medical explanation for positive amphetamine tests in a workplace drug testing

There are 14 drugs which are metabolized to amphetamine or methamphetamine (and then also to amphetamine) and may lead to positive test results with amphetamine/methamphetamine in workplace drug testing. These drugs include amphetaminil, benzphetamine, clobenzorex, dimethylamphetamine, ethylamphetamine, famprofazone, fencamine, fenethylline, fenproporex, fenfenorex, mefenorex, mesocarb, selegiline, and prenylamine [34]. See Table 9.2 for common drugs containing amphetamine/methamphetamine or which are metabolized to methamphetamine or amphetamine.

Table 9.2 Drugs that contain amphetamine or methamphetamine or are metabolized to amphetamine or methamphetamine

Active ingredient	Brand names
Amphetamine	Adderal®l, Biphetamine®, Dexedrine®, Dextrostat®
D-Methamphetamine	Desoxyn®
L-Amphetamine	Vicks® inhaler (non-prescription medication)
Active ingredient metabolized to amphetamine	
Amphetaminil	Aponeuron®, Clobenzorex Aselin®, Asenlix®, Dinintel®, Finedal®, Rexigen®
Clobenzorex	Asenlix®, Finedal®, Rexigen®
Ethyl amphetamine	Apetinil®
Fenethylline	Captagon®
Fenproporex	Falagan®, Lipoli®n (mostly replaced by other drugs or withdrawn due to toxicity)
Mefenorex	Rondimen®, Pondinil®, Anexate®
Prenylamine	Segontin®, Segentine®
Active ingredient metabolized to methamphetamine	
Benzphetamine	Didrex®
Famprofazone	Gewodin®
Furfenorex	Withdrawn due to abuse potential.
Selegiline	Carbex®, Deprenyl®, Eldepryl®

Cody et al. reported urinary amphetamine levels in five volunteers who ingested 20 mg each of Adderall tablets. The peak amphetamine concentrations ranged from 2,645 to 5,948 ng/mL and a positive amphetamine concentration above the GC/MS confirmation level of 500 ng/mL was observed up to 47.5 h post ingestion. As expected, both D and L isomers of amphetamine were observed in urine which distinguished the profile from illicit use of amphetamine which contains mostly D isomer. However, another amphetamine containing drug Dexedrine contains only D isomer [35]. In another study by Cody and Valtier a single dose of benzphetamine was given to ten subjects (seven male, three female) and urine samples were collected for the next 7 days. GC/MS analysis of urine specimens revealed that three out of ten subjects did not have a single urine sample where the amphetamine concentration exceeded the GC/MS cut-off value of 500 ng/mL, but other subjects showed positive amphetamine specimens at that cut-off. Two subjects excreted more methamphetamine than amphetamine but other eight subjects excreted more amphetamine than methamphetamine [36]. In another study, volunteers ingested 120 mg oral dose of prenylamine which is also known to metabolize to amphetamine. The immunoassay screening of amphetamine using the FPIA amphetamine/methamphetamine assay (Abbott Laboratories, Abbott Park, IL) showed wide variations in amphetamine levels as a urine specimen collected from one volunteer showed amphetamine concentration of 3,200 ng/mL while a urine specimen collected from another volunteer provided a negative screen for amphetamine/methamphetamine. The GC/MS analysis confirmed the presence of both D and L isomer of amphetamine because prenylamine is marketed as a racemic mixture (mixture of both D and L isomer) [37]. Selegiline, a drug used in treating Parkinson's disease, is metabolized to L-methamphetamine which is further metabolized to L-amphetamine. Given stereospecificity of antibody used in designing of immunoassays for screening of amphetamine/methamphetamine in urine, a low dosage of selegiline should not produce a positive screening result. Nevertheless, positive immunoassay screening results using the FPIA amphetamine/methamphetamine assay (Abbott Laboratories, Abbott Park, IL) were observed up to 2 days following ingestion of a 10-mg selegiline tablet. However, mostly L isomers of both methamphetamine and amphetamine were detected in urine which was distinguished from ingestion of selegiline for illicit use of methamphetamine because, in the case of illicit use of methamphetamine, mostly D isomer is present in the urine specimen [38].

9 Case Studies

The following cases were taken from MRO Case Studies, a publication of SAMHSA (Health and Human Services of the US Government) [39].

Case Report 1: The laboratory reported a methamphetamine concentration of 950 ng/mL and amphetamine concentration of 245 ng/mL. During the interview, the donor denied any prescription medication but disclosed that he used Vicks®

inhaler. The MRO requested the laboratory to perform a chiral analysis and it was found that 90% of the isomers were D isomer. Since Vicks® inhaler contains mainly L-methamphetamine, such high amount of D isomer cannot come from the use of inhaler. The MRO reported the test positive for methamphetamine.

Case Report 2: The laboratory reported methamphetamine concentration of 1,250 ng/mL and amphetamine concentration of 225 ng/mL. During the interview the donor reported that he used Vicks® inhaler and also Valium (diazepam). When the laboratory performed the chiral analysis, 95% of the methamphetamine and amphetamine present were L isomers, which was consistent with the use of Vicks® inhaler. The MRO reported the test as negative because the Federal workplace drug testing program does not mandate testing of benzodiazepines. The legitimate use of prescription us of Valium is a confidential medical information and may not be disclosed to the agency.

10 Conclusions

Over-the-counter cold medications may cause false positive immunoassay amphetamine/methamphetamine screens but GC/MS certainly should distinguish such interfering compounds from either methamphetamine or methamphetamine. On the other hand, several prescription medications contain amphetamine or methamphetamine and 14 medications are metabolized to either methamphetamine or amphetamine. Using these medications may cause positive amphetamine/methamphetamine confirmation but, after producing a valid prescription, the MRO can determine whether positive test could be related to use of such prescription drugs.

References

1. Zapata LB, Hills SD, Marchbanks PA, Curtis KM et al. Methamphetamine use is independently associated with risky sexual behavior and adolescent pregnancy. J Sch Health 2008; 78: 641–658.
2. Redback CJ, Shoptaw S, Grella CE. Methamphetamine use trends among street recruited gay and bisexual males from 1999 to 2007. J Urbal Health 2008; 85: 874–879.
3. Pedersen W, Skrondal A. Ecstasy and new patterns of drug use: a normal population study. Addiction 1999; 94: 1695–1706.
4. Moore KA. Amphetamines/sympathomimetic amines. In: B Levine ed. Principles of Forensic Toxicology. AACC Press, Washington, D.C, 2003, pp. 341–348.
5. Grinstead GF. Ranitidine and high concentrations of phenylpropanolamine cross react in the EMIT monoclonal amphetamine/methamphetamine assay. Clin Chem 1989; 35: 1998–1999.
6. Poklis A. Unavailability of drug metabolite reference material to evaluate false-positive results for monoclonal EMIT-d.a.u. assay of amphetamine. Clin Chem 1992; 38: 2580.
7. Caplan YH, Levine B, Goldberger B. Fluorescence polarization immunoassay evaluated for screening for amphetamine and methamphetamine in urine. Clin Chem 1987; 33: 1200–1202.
8. Papa P, Rocchi L, Mainardi C, Donzelli G. Buflomedil interference with the monoclonal EMIT d.a.u. amphetamine/methamphetamine immunoassay. Eur J Clin Chem Clin Biochem 1997; 35: 369–370.

9. Olsen KM, Gulliksen M, Christophersen AS. Metabolites of chlorpromazine and brompheniramine may cause false-positive urine amphetamine results with monoclonal EMIT d.a.u. immunoassay. Clin Chem 1992; 38: 611–612.
10. Smith-Kielland A, Olsen KM, Christophersen AS. False-positive results with EMIT II amphetamine/methamphetamine assay in users of common psychotropic drugs. Clin Chem 1995; 41: 951–952.
11. Dasgupta A, Saldana S, Kinnaman G, Smith M, Johansen K. Analytical performance evaluation of EMIT II monoclonal amphetamine/methamphetamine assay: more specificity than EMIT d.a.u. monoclonal amphetamine/ methamphetamine assay. Clin Chem 1993; 39: 104–108.
12. Joseph R, Dickerson S, Willis R, Frankenfield D, Cone EJ, Smith DR. Interference by nonsteroidal anti-inflammatory drugs in EMIT and TDx assays for drugs of abuse. J Anal Toxicol 1995; 19: 13–17.
13. Nice A, Maturen A. False-positive urine amphetamine screen with ritodrine. Clin Chem 1989; 35: 1542–1543.
14. Jones R, Klette K, Kuhlman JJ, Levine B, Smith ML, Watson CV, Selavka CM. Trimethobenzamide cross-reacts in immunoassays of amphetamine-methamphetamine. Clin Chem 1993; 39: 699–700.
15. Kozer E, Verjee Z, Koren G. Misdiagnosis of a mexiletine overdose because of a nonspecific result of urinary toxicology screening. New Eng J Med 2000; 343(26): 1971.
16. Schmolke M, Hallbach J, Guder WG. False-positive results for urine amphetamine and opiate immunoassays in a patient intoxicated with perazine. Clin Chem 1996; 42: 1725–1726.
17. Takayasu T, Ohshima T, Nishigami J, Kondo T et al. Screening and determination of methamphetamine and amphetamine in the blood, urine and stomach contents in emergency medical care and autopsy cases. J Clin Forensic Med 1995; 2: 25–33.
18. Shindelman J, Mahal J, Hemphill G, Pizzo P, Coty WA. Development and evaluation of an improved method for screening of amphetamines. J Anal Toxicol 1999; 23: 506–510.
19. Woodworth A, Saunders AN, Koenig JW, Moyer TP, Turk J, Dietzen DJ. Differentiation of amphetamine/methamphetamine and other cross-immunoreactive sympathomimetic amines in urine samples by serial dilution testing. Clin Chem 2006; 52: 743–746.
20. Melanson SE, Lee-Lewandrowski E, Griggs DA, Long WH et al. Reduced interference by phenothiazine in amphetamine drug of abuse immunoassay. Arch Pathol Lab Med 2006; 130: 1834–1838.
21. Cooke BJ. Chirality of methamphetamine and amphetamine from workplace urine samples. J Anal Toxicol 1994; 18: 49–51.
22. Poklis A, Jortani SA, Brown CS, Crooks CR. Response of the EMIT II amphetamine/methamphetamine assay to specimens collected following use of Vicks® inhalers. J Anal Toxicol 1993; 17: 284–286.
23. Poklis A, Moore KA. Stereoselectivity of TDxADx/FLx amphetamine/ methamphetamine II immunoassay-response of urine specimens following nasal inhaler use. J Toxicol Clin Toxicol 1995; 33: 35–41.
24. MRO Case Studies (Health and Human Services of the US Government) 2005: http://workplace.samhsa.gov/DrugTesting/Files_Drug_Testing/MROs/MRO%20Case%20Studies%20-%20Ferbruary%202005.pdf
25. Haller CA, Benowitz NL. Adverse and central nervous system events associated with dietary supplements containing ephedra alkaloids. N Eng J Med 2000; 343: 1833–1838.
26. Nguyen MH, Ormiston T, Kurani S, Woo DK. Amphetamine lacing of an Internet marketed nutraceutical. Mayo Clinic Proc 2006; 81: 1627–1629.
27. Haaz S, Fontaine KB, Cutter G, Limdi N et al. Citrus aurantium and synephrine alkaloids in the treatment of overweight and obesity: an update. Obes Res 2006; 7: 79–88.
28. Nguyen DT, Bui LT, Ambrose PJ. Response of CEDIA amphetamines assay after a single dose of bitter orange. Ther Drug Monit 2006; 28: 252–254.

29. Hornbeck CL, Carrig JE, Czarny RJ. Detection of a GC/MS artifact peak as methamphetamine. J Anal Toxicol 1993; 17: 257–263.
30. ElSohly MA, Stanford DF, Sherman D, Shah H, Bernot D, Turner CE. A procedure for eliminating interferences from ephedrine and related compounds in the GC/MS analysis of amphetamine and methamphetamine. J Anal Toxicol 1992; 16: 109–111.
31. Dasgupta A, Gardner C. Distinguishing amphetamine and methamphetamine from other interfering sympathomimetic amines after various fluoro derivatization and analysis by gas chromatography-chemical ionization mass spectrometry. J Forensic Sci 1995; 40: 1077–1081.
32. Elliott S, Burgers V. Investigative implications of instability and metabolism of mebeverine. J Anal Toxicol 2006; 30: 91–97.
33. Kraemer T, Wenning R, Maurer HH. The antispasmodic drug mebeverine leads to positive amphetamine results by fluorescence polarization immunoassay (FPIA)-studies on the toxicological analysis of urine by FPIA and GC–MS. J Anal Toxicol 2001; 25: 333–338.
34. Musshoff F. Illegal or legitimate use? Precursor compounds to amphetamine and methamphetamine. Drug Metab Rev 2000; 32: 15–44.
35. Cody JT, Valtier S, Nelson SL. Amphetamine enantiomer excretion profile following administration of Adderall. J Anal Toxicol 2003; 27: 485–492.
36. Cody JT, Valtier S. Detection of amphetamine and methamphetamine following administration of benzphetamine. J Anal Toxicol 1998; 22: 299–309.
37. Kraemer T, Roditis SK, Peters FT, Maurer HH. Amphetamine concentrations in human urine following single-dose administration of calcium antagonist prenylamine-studies using fluorescence polarization immunoassay (FPIA) and GC–MS. J Anal Toxicol 2003; 27: 68–73.
38. Maurer HH, Kraemer T. Toxicological detection of selegiline and its metabolites in urine using fluorescence polarization immunoassay (FPIA) and gas chromatography-mass spectrometry (GC–MS) and differentiation by enantioselective GC–MS of the intake of selegiline from abuse of methamphetamine or amphetamine. Arch Toxicol 1992; 66: 675–678.
39. MRO Case Studies (Health and Human Services of the US Government) 2005: http:// workplace.samhsa.gov/ DrugTesting/Files_Drug_Testing/MROs/MRO%20Case%20Studies%20-%20Ferbruary%202005.pdf
40. Moore KA. Amphetamines/sympathomimetic amines. In: Levine B ed. Principles of Forensic Toxicology, Revised and Updated. 2nd ed. AACC Press, Washington, DC, 2006, 277–296.

Chapter 10
Analytical True Positives in Workplace Drugs Testings Due to Use of Prescription and OTC Medications

Abstract Analytical true positive workplace drug testing results due to use of prescription medication or OTC (over-the-counter) medication do occur. Amphetamine positive result due to prescription medication was discussed in Chap. 9. Prescription use of any benzodiazepine may cause positive test results although benzodiazepine is not one of the SAMHSA drugs. Topical use of cocaine may cause positive results in workplace drug testing. Many pain medications contain opiates and use of such medication leads to false positive opiate tests. Marinol is synthetic marijuana which is metabolized in the same way as marijuana and can cause positive marijuana results in workplace drug testing.

Keywords Marijuana · Marinol · True positive

1 Introduction

Many prescription drugs are also abused in a non-medical setting but legal use of a prescription medication may cause positive test results in workplace drug testing. Abuse of many prescription medications is a serious public health as well as a public safety issue. All statistics show that abuse of prescription drugs is on the rise in the United States with increasing emergency room visits and accidental deaths from abuse of prescription drugs. Current non-medical abuse of prescription drugs among young adults aged 18–25 years increased from 5.4% in 2002 to 6.3% in 2005. Statistics further show that abuse of prescription drugs is only second to marijuana abuse and three times more people abuse prescription drugs than abuse cocaine [1]. Americans, constituting only 4.6% of the world population, consume 80% of the global supply of opiates, 99% of the worlds' hydrocodone supply and abuse two thirds of the world's illicit drugs. It has been documented that 80% of American high school students (or 11 million teens) and 44% of middle school students (or 5 million teens) have personally witnessed, on their school grounds, illegal drug dealing, illegal drug use, and other activities related to illicit drug use. The results of

A. Dasgupta, *Beating Drug Tests and Defending Positive Results*,
DOI 10.1007/978-1-60761-527-9_10, © Springer Science+Business Media, LLC 2010

the 2006 National Survey on Drug Use have shown that 2.8% of the United States population (estimated at 7.0 million people) age 12 or older had non-medically used prescription medication in the past month while 6.6 % of the population (estimated 16.387 million people) had abused prescription medication during the past 1 year of the survey. It had been estimated that 20.3% of the population (49.8 million people) had abused prescription drugs during their lifetime [2]. Wunsch et al. reported that, in rural Virginia, drug overdose death increased 300% from 1997 to 2003. In addition, prescription opioids, antidepressants, and benzodiazepines were more prevalent than illicit drugs [3].

Because of widespread abuse of prescription medication, it is important to differentiate the cause of proper medical use of a drug vs non-medical abuse. If a workplace drug testing is positive for a prescription drug, then the medical review officer (MRO) must investigate the cause. A valid prescription for the drug and expected concentration of that drug in the urine specimen may explain the positive test result. However, a lack of prescription or an abnormally high concentration of the drug may indicate abuse.

2 Prescription Medications Containing Benzodiazepines

In the SAMHSA five drug panels, the presence of any benzodiazepines is not tested for. However, private employers may test for the presence of benzodiazepines in urine in employees as a part of their workplace drug testing program. Benzodiazepines are one of the most frequently prescribed drugs in the United States and are used as tranquilizers, muscle relaxants, anticonvulsants, and also for treating symptoms of anxiety. There are more than 50 different types of benzodiazepines but not all drugs are available in the United States. In the United States approximately 15 different benzodiazepines are prescribed while the most commonly prescribed benzodiazepines are diazepam, temazepam, alprazolam, lorazepam, and clonazepam. Some of the drugs in this class such as estazolam, temazepam, halazepam and quazepam are derivatives of benzodiazepine. Several drugs in the benzodiazepine class, for example flurazepam, is short acting while diazepam, alprazolam, and other related drugs are long acting benzodiazepines. Commonly prescribed short and long acting benzodiazepines are listed in Table 10.1.

Usually immunoassay screening for benzodiazepines recognized the presence of common drugs and metabolites after medical use or abuse. Many immunoassays target oxazepam, the common metabolite of several benzodiazepines. The On-Line Benzodiazepine Plus assay by Roche Diagnostics (Indianapolis, IN) recognized the presence of 22 common benzodiazepines and their metabolites including alprazolam, chlordiazepoxide, clonazepam, clorazepate, diazepam, estazolam, flunitrazepam, halazepam, lorazepam, midazolam, nitrazepam, oxazepam, temazepam, and triazolam. DeRienz et al. evaluated four commercial immunoassays at a 200 ng/mL cut-off concentration for screening of benzodiazepines in urine

Table 10.1 Commonly prescribed short and long acting benzodiazepines

Short acting benzodiazepines		
Estazolam	Flurazepam	Temazepam
Triazolam	Midazolam	
Long acting benzodiazepines		
Alprazolam	Chlordiazepoxide	Clorazepate
Clonazepam	Diazepam	Halazepam
Lorazepam	Nitrazepam	Prazepam
Oxazepam	Quazepam	

specimens and concluded that Microgenics CEDIA high sensitivity assay with beta-glucuronidase showed the highest positive screening rate as well as the highest confirmation rate compared to the other threes assays (Roche Benzodiazepine Plus KIMS assay, Microgenics CEDIA benzodiazepine assay and Microgenics DRI reagent ready benzodiazepine assays) [4]. Because many benzodiazepine metabolites are conjugated, hydrolysis with beta-glucuronidase often increases sensitivity of a benzodiazepine screening assay. In another article, the authors investigated performance of Roche Online KIMS (kinetic interaction of microparticle in solution) benzodiazepine immunoassays with or without beta-glucuronidase treatment and observed that, with hydrolysis, temazepam, oxazepam, and lorazepam metabolites produce cross-reactivities of 25, 15, and 20% respectively. Without hydrolysis, the cross-reactivity was less than 1%. The authors concluded that automatic addition of beta-glucuronidase in this assay can be well adopted for rapid detection of benzodiazepines and their metabolites in urine specimens [5].

Oxaprozin is a non-steroidal antiinflammatory drug which cross-reacts with various benzodiazepines immunoassays. Fraser and Jowell reported that oxaprozin causes false positive screening results with three benzodiazepine immunoassays; EMIT d.a.u. (Dade Behring), FPIA (Abbott Laboratories) and CEDIA (Microgenics). When 12 subjects received a single standard dose of oxaprozin (1,200 mg), all 36 urine specimens collected from these 12 subjects demonstrated positive screen for the presence of benzodiazepines [6]. However, zolpidem (Ambien), a sleeping aid which has some structural similarity with various benzodiazepines, does not cross react with the two most commonly used immunoassays (Syva EMIT II and Abbott ADx) urine drug screening assay [7].

Because of the wide diversity of this class of drug, immunoassay positive specimens are usually confirmed by GC/MS for common drugs in this class including oxazepam, diazepam, temazepam, and alprazolam. ElSohly et al. analyzed benzodiazepines in 156 urine specimens from alleged victims of drug facilitated sexual assault and observed that oxazepam was confirmed in 50% of the specimens followed by nordiazepam (48%), temazepam (43%), and diazepam (40%) while the presence of alprazolam was confirmed in 21.8% and lorazepam in 15.4% of the specimens [8]. Although GC/MS is commonly used for confirmation of the presence of benzodiazepines in urine specimens, recently ElSohly et al. described a protocol for simultaneous analysis of 325 benzodiazepines in urine using liquid chromatography-time of flight mass spectrometry [9]. Medical use of many benzodiazepines produces positive drug testing results but, based on moderate urinary concentration of benzodiazepine, it is difficult to differentiate non-medical use of benzodiazepine from abuse.

3 Topical Use of Cocaine and Workplace Drug Testing

Cocaine is unstable in the human body and is rapidly converted into benzoylecgonine and ecgonine methyl ester. There is a popular belief in the lay Internet based literature that use of the antibiotic amoxicillin may cause false positive cocaine test result. However, there is no scientific basis for this claim. Reisfield et al. using 33 volunteers clearly demonstrated that amoxicillin is unlikely to produce false positive urine screens for cocaine metabolites [10].

Cocaine is used infrequently as a local anesthetic in ear, nose, and throat surgery and is sometimes also administered topically during ophthalmitic procedures. Positive drug testing results for cocaine (as benzoylecgonine) may be encountered in subjects who have undergone such procedures. After an otolaryngologic procedure where cocaine is used as an anesthetic, a patient may test positive for up to 72 h after and cocaine metabolite can also be detected in the urine specimen of the physician who performed the procedure [11]. However, Kavanagh et al. using 11 medical staff members who were exposed to cocaine hydrochloride by means of aerosol and cutaneous application concluded that it would be unlikely that a single passive exposure to cocaine could produce a positive cocaine test in medical personnel [12].

Jacobson et al. studied the effect of use of ophthalmic solution containing cocaine on urine excretion of benzoylecgonine in patients. Out of 50 subjects studied, 47 subjects (94%) demonstrated positive screening results for cocaine (as benzoylecgonine) 4–6 h after receiving eye drops. In addition, 35 subjects (70%) showed positive results 24 h after receiving eye drops containing cocaine. The authors conclude that ophthalmic administration of cocaine may cause positive test results for up to 2 days after procedure [13]. Cocaine is also used in lacrimal surgery. In one study using 12 patients, the authors reported that all 12 patients tested positive for benzoylecgonine (measured by the Syva EMIT test) for 24 h, 9 patients after 48 h and 3 patients even after 72 h [14]. The combination of tetracaine, adrenalin, and cocaine is used as a topical anesthetic during the suture of simple skin lacerations. Application of such topical anesthetics also produces positive urine tests for cocaine for up to 2 days [15].

Novocain, although synthetically derived from cocaine, has a distinct structural difference from cocaine and the metabolite of cocaine (benzoylecgonine). Therefore use of Novocain during dental procedure or use of other anesthetic agents including benzocaine, tetracaine, and lidocaine should not cause false positive cocaine test results in urine drugs of abuse testing.

4 Prescription Opiates and Workplace Drug Testing

Several prescription medications for treating moderate to severe pain contain morphine, codeine, hydrocodone, oxycodone, or related opioid such as oxymorphone. Methadone which is a synthetic opiate is used as an agent in drug rehabilitation centers. Unfortunately, methadone is also abused. Another synthetic opiate fentanyl is used for severe pain management. Duragesic fentanyl patch is also employed to treat pain. Although using morphine or codeine containing medication would results in positive opiate screening as well as confirmation test result in the urine specimen, other synthetic or semi-synthetic opiates have variable cross-reactivity with opiate immunoassay screening test.

Opiate immunoassays are designed to detect morphine and codeine. Most commercially available immunoassays have relatively high cross-reactivity with hydrocodone and hydromorphone but usually poor cross reactivity with oxycodone. For example Roche On-Line opiate immunoassay (Roche Diagnostics, Indianapolis, IN) has less than 4% cross-reactivity with oxycodone but the corresponding cross-reactivities with hydromorphone and hydrocodone are 21 and 28% respective (package insert). EMIT d.a.u. and EMIT II Plus opiate assay (Dade Behring, Deerfield, IL) have 6.7 and 5.6% cross-reactivity with oxycodone respectively. Smith et al. reported that, when a single dose of hydrocodone, hydromorphone, oxycodone, or oxymorphone was administered to volunteers, both parent drugs and O-demethylated metabolites were excreted with peak concentrations reached within 8 h and then declined to below 300 ng/mL within 24–48 h. Immunoassay screening for opiates using both EMIT (Dade Behring) and FPIA (Abbott Laboratories) detected hydromorphone, hydrocodone, and oxycodone between 6 and 24 h after ingestion of the respective drug using a cut-off opiate concentration of 300 ng/mL but neither assay detected the presence of oxymorphone. The authors concluded that urine specimens containing low to moderate concentrations of hydromorphone, hydrocodone, oxycodone, and oxymorphone will likely test negative using conventional immunoassays for screening of opiates [16]. Chemical structures of hydromorphone and oxycodone are given in Fig. 10.1.

Because of lack of cross-reactivity of oxycodone with commercially available opiate assays, specific immunoassays with oxycodone as the target analyte has been developed. Dunn et al. analyzed 437 urine specimens collected from 137 patients undergoing a methadone maintenance program in order to determine whether any such patients were using oxycodone. Using the EMIT opiate assay, only 6% of specimens (20 out of 437 specimens) showed positive response while using a specific oxycodone test strip 19% of specimens (83 out of 437 specimens) showed positive response [17]. In addition to oxycodone, opiate immunoassays are usually unable to detect methadone and fentanyl. Specific immunoassay for detecting either methadone or its major metabolite is commercially available.

Ethylmorphine, which is used in many countries as an antitussive agent, is metabolized to morphine. Ingestion of ethylmorphine produces 100% positive test results with opiate screening in urine specimens using the EMIT (Dade Behring, Deerfield, IL) assay during the first 24 h of administration of the drug. Both ethylmorphine

Fig. 10.1 Chemical structure of oxycodone and hydromorphone

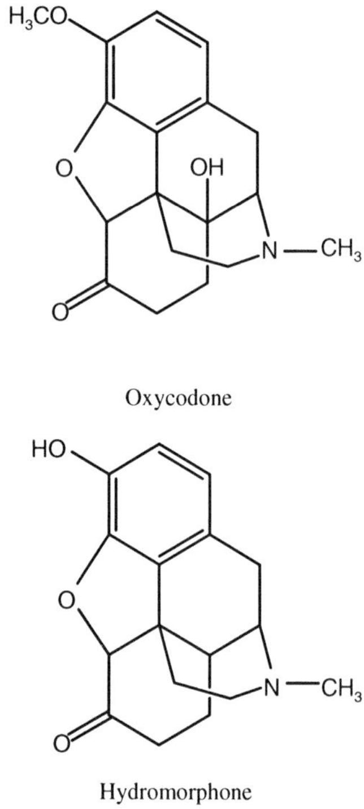

and morphine were detected in urine specimens while morphine was formed from ethylmorphine at a highly variable rate [18].

If a positive test result is obtained due to use of a prescription opiate, then the medical review officer (MRO) must verify that information and determine whether urine drug level is consistent with the use of a prescription opiate. For example, if 6-acetylmorphine is confirmed in a urine specimen it can only occur due to heroin abuse and not from taking any opiate containing medication or poppy seed containing food. Hydrocodone is metabolized to hydromorphone, while oxycodone is metabolized to oxymorphone.

4.1 Detection of Hydromorphone After Medical Use of Morphine

Hydromorphone is a minor metabolite of morphine that may be present in a patient taking morphine for pain control. Therefore, the presence of hydromorphone in a urine specimen along with high morphine concentration in a patient taking only morphine is not an indication of hydromorphone abuse. Wasan et al. reported that hydromorphone was present in urine specimens of 21 out of 32 patients (66%) who were not exposed to hydromorphone. Positive morphine was encountered more in females and also in those individuals taking higher dosages of morphine. Morphine dosage, gender, urinary morphine concentration and genetic factors all play important roles in determining the presence of morphine in urine [19]. Cone et al. also detected hydromorphone in urine specimens of patients receiving high doses of morphine. The ratio of hydromorphone to morphine ranged from 0.2 to 2.2%. However, oxymorphone was not detected in any urine specimen analyzed by the authors. The authors concluded that, although hydromorphone is a minor metabolite of morphine, oxymorphone is not a metabolite of morphine or hydromorphone [20]. Therefore, the presence of oxymorphone in the absence of a valid prescription for oxymorphone indicates drug abuse. A list of narcotics that are not metabolized to either morphine or codeine is given in Table 10.2.

Table 10.2 Narcotics that are not metabolized to either morphine or codeine

Hydromorphone	Hydrocodone	Dihydrocodeine
Oxycodone	Oxymorphone	Propoxyphene
Methadone	Meperidine	Fentanyl
Pentazocine	Buprenorphine	

4.2 Detection of Hydrocodone After Medical Use of Codeine

Allegation of illicit hydrocodone had been made against an individual who is taking oral codeine based on a physician's prescription but denying any abuse of hydrocodone. Olyer et al. investigated whether hydrocodone can be detected in urine following prescription use of codeine. In the first study, five volunteers ingested 60 mg (per 70 kg/day) and 70 mg (per 70 kg/day) on separate days. Codeine was detected in the first post codeine urine specimen for all subjects and the peak concentration appeared at 2–5 h, ranging from 1,475 to 61,695 ng/mL. Hydrocodone was initially detected at 6–11 h post ingestion of codeine and peaked at 10–18 h. The peak concentration of hydrocodone varied from 32 to 135 ng/mL. When a postoperative patient took 960 mg/day of codeine based on the physician's prescription, codeine and hydrocodone were detected in all urine specimens collected from the patient. The concentration of codeine varied from 2,099 to 4,020 ng/mL while the concentration of hydrocodone varied from 47 to 129 ng/mL. Analysis of the codeine preparation the patient was taking, showed no presence of hydrocodone. The authors concluded that hydrocodone can be produced as the minor metabolite of morphine and can be present at a concentration as high as 11% of the codeine concentration. Therefore, the detection of a minor amount of hydrocodone in urine containing high concentration of codeine should not be interpreted as evidence of hydrocodone abuse in an individual [21].

5 OTC Opiates and Workplace Drug Testing

Codeine is available by prescription only in most parts of the United States, although several over-the-counter (OTC) products containing codeine are available in some states. The amount of codeine is usually 8 mg per dose or less. With liquid cough preparations the recommended level is only 3.2 mg/mL. Some codeine containing products are available as OTC drugs in most provinces of Canada. In Japan, OTC drug SS-BRON, an antitussive, contains dihydrocodeine, methyl ephedrine, chlorpheniramine, and caffeine. Although the level of morphine or codeine is relatively small in these products compared to prescription opiates, nevertheless use of such products may also cause positive opiate test results especially in the case of private workplace drug testing where the employer is using 300 ng/mL as the cut-off concentration. A list of OTC products containing morphine or codeine is given in Table 10.3. In addition, these OTC drugs can also be abused. Murao et al. reported intoxication with OTC drug SS-BRON in a 35-year-old man requiring hospitalization [22].

Table 10.3 Over-the-counter (OTC) codeine and morphine containing products

Drug	Brand names
Morphine	Donnagel-PG®[a] Quiagel®[a] Infantol Pink®[a] Kaodene with Paregoric®[a]
Codeine	Kaodene with Codeine®[a]
Acetaminophen with Codeine	Available OTC in certain parts of CANADA

[a]Source of information: Medical Review Officer Manual for Federal Agency Workplace Drug Testing

6 Marinol and Workplace Drug Testing

Marijuana is tested in urine specimens as its major metabolite 11-nor-9-carboxy-Δ^9-tetrahydrocannabinol (THC–COOH). Immunoassay screenings of marijuana metabolite in urine specimens produce reliable result with very few false positives. In one recent article, the author observed that the EMIT assay for marijuana has only a 3% false positive rate [23]. Antiretroviral therapy with efavirenz in patients with AIDS may cause false positive tests for marijuana metabolite (using 50 ng/mL as cut-off level) using CEDIA DAU Multi-level THC (Microgenics Corporation), Triage Drug Screen (Biosite Corporation, San Diego, CA), and Cannabinoid THCA/CTHC Direct ELISA kit (Immunalysis Corporation). In contrast, no false positive test result was observed using EMIT assay (Dade Behring), FPIA assay

(Abbott Laboratories) and Intercept Microplate point of care testing device (OraSure Technology). It was speculated that a false positive result was due to the metabolite of efavirenz (efavirenz-8-glucuronide) [24].

Although marijuana is a schedule I drug, a synthetic tetrahydrocannabinol (dronabinol) is sold under the trade name of Marinol for treating nausea and vomiting in cancer patients undergoing chemotherapy, and also as an appetite stimulant to patients with AIDS. Because Marinol is also converted into marijuana metabolite (THC-COOH), use of Marinol produces a positive test for marijuana metabolites in drugs of abuse testing. However, delta-9-tetrahydrocannabivarin (THCV) which is a natural constituent of cannabis product is absent in dronabinol. THVC is metabolized by the human liver into THCV-COOH and the presence of this metabolite in addition to THC–COOH in urine indicates abuse of marijuana rather than prescription use of dronabinol [25].

6.1 Marijuana and Chocolate

Anandamide, also known as *N*-arachidonoylethanolamine, is an endogenous cannabinoid neurotransmitter found in animals and in humans, mostly in the brain. This chemical is responsible for the narcotic effect of marijuana. Anandamide along with *N*-linoleylethanolamine and *N*-oleylethanolamine are also found in chocolates. The latter two compounds in an animal model inhibit hydrolysis of anandamide, thus prolonging the high effect [26]. Chocolate is also believed to enhance the effect of marijuana [27]. A defendant's lawyer, in order to clear the accused of smoking or dealing with marijuana after he was found positive for marijuana in a routine immunoassay screening test, used consumption of massive amounts of chocolate by the accused as a defense. Because chocolates contain anandamide and mimics the effect of marijuana, the lawyer claimed that the positive test result for marijuana in the urine was due to ingestion of massive amounts of chocolate. Tytgat et al. synthesized *N*-oleyl- and *N*-linoleoylethanolaminde and spiked these compounds along with *N*-arachidonoylethanolamide in urine but did not observe any false positive marijuana test result using an immunoassay [28]. This is expected because these compounds found in chocolate are structurally very different from THC–COOH.

7 Conclusions

Various prescription medications may lead to positive analytical test results in workplace drug testing and the MRO should be able to determine whether the positive test result could be related to proper use of a prescription drug or from abuse. Various benzodiazepines are used medically in the United States and, based on benzodiazepine concentrations in the urine specimen, it may be difficult to separate a medical use from abuse unless the drug concentration is very high. Topical use of morphine as a local anesthetic may cause positive cocaine test results in workplace drug testing. Many prescription opiate drugs may cause positive opiate test results. In addition, prescription use of morphine may result in a small amount of hydromorphone level in the urine along with high morphine concentration. Similarly, the presence of a small amount of hydrocodone in the presence of high codeine does not indicate hydrocodone abuse. Use of Marinol would cause a positive marijuana test.

References

1. Manchikanti L. National drug control policy and prescription drug abuse: facts and fallacies. Pain Physician 2007; 10: 399–424.
2. Manchikanti L, Singh A. Therapeutic opioids: a ten year perspective on the complexities and complications of the escalating use, abuse, and nonmedical use of opioids. Pain Physician 2008; 11(2 Suppl): S63–S88.
3. Wunsch MJ, Nakamoto K, Behonick G, Massello W. Opioid deaths in rural Virginia: a description of the high prevalence of accidental fatalities involving prescribed medications. Am J Addict 2009; 18: 5–14.
4. DeRienz RT, Holler JM, Manos ME, Jemionek J et al. Evaluation of four immunoassays screening kits for the detection of benzodiazepines in urine. J Anal Toxicol 2008; 32: 433–437.
5. Klette KL, Wiegand RF, Horn CK, Stout PR et al. Urine benzodiazepine screening using Roche Online KIMS immunoassay with beta-glucuronidase hydrolysis and confirmation by gas chromatography-mass spectrometry. J Anal Toxicol 2005; 19: 193–200.
6. Fraser AD, Jowell P. Oxaprozin cross-reactivity in three commercial immunoassays for benzodiazepines in urine. J Anal Toxicol 1998; 22: 50–54.
7. Piergies AA, Sainati S, Roth-Schechter B. Lack of cross-reactivity of Ambien (zolpidem) with drugs in standard urine drug screens. Arch Pathol Lab med 1997; 121: 392–394.
8. ElSohly MA, Gul W, Murphy TP, Avula B. LC-(TOF) MS analysis of benzodiazepines in urine from alleged victims of drug facilitated sexual assault. J Anal Toxicol 2007; 31: 505–514.
9. ElSohly MA, Gul W, Avula B, Murphy TP et al. Simultaneous analysis of thirty five benzodiazepines using liquid chromatography-mass spectrometry time of flight. J Anal Toxicol 2008; 32: 547–561.
10. Reisfield GM, Haddad J, Wilson GR, Johannsen LM et al. Failure of amoxicillin to produce false-positive urine screens for cocaine metabolite. J Anal Toxicol 2008; 32: 315–318.
11. Bruns AD, Zeiske LA, Jacobs AJ. Analysis of the cocaine metabolite in the urine of patients and physicians during clinical use. Otolaryngol Head Neck Surg 1994; 111: 722–726.
12. Kavanagh KT, Maijub AG, Brown JR. Passive exposure to cocaine in medical personnel and its effect on urine drug screening test. Otolaryngol Head Neck Surg 1992; 107: 363–366.
13. Jacobson DM, Berg R, Grinstead GF, Kruse JR. Duration of positive urine for cocaine metabolite after ophthalmic administration: implications for testing patients with suspected Horner syndrome using ophthalmic cocaine. Am J Ophthalmol 2001; 131: 742–747.
14. Patrinely JR, Cruz OA, Reyna GS, King JW. The use of cocaine as an anesthetic in lacrimal surgery. J Anal Toxicol 1994; 18: 54–56.
15. Altieri M, Bogema S, Schwartz RH. TAC topical anesthesia produces positive urine test for cocaine. Ann Emerg Med 1990; 19: 577–579.
16. Smith ML, Hughes RO, Levine B, Dickerson S et al. Forensic drug testing for opiates. VI. Urine testing for hydromorphone, hydrocodone, oxymorphone and oxycodone with commercial opiate immunoassays and gas chromatography-mass spectrometry. J Anal Toxicol 1995; 19: 18–26.
17. Dunn KE, Sigmon SC, McGee MR, Heil MR et al. Evaluation of ongoing oxycodone abuse among methadone maintained patients. J Subst Abuse Test 2008; 35: 451–456.

18. Popa C, Beck O, Brodin K. Morphine formation from ethylmorphine: implications for drugs of abuse testing in urine. J Anal Toxicol 1998; 22: 142–147.
19. Wasam AD, Michna E, Janfaza D, Greenfield S et al. Interpreting urine drug tests: prevalence of morphine metabolism to hydromorphone in chronic pain patients treated with morphine. Pain Med 2008; 9: 918–923.
20. Cone EJ, Caplan YH, Moser F, Robert T et al. Evidence that morphine is metabolized to hydromorphone but not to oxymorphone. J Anal Toxicol 2008; 32(4): 319–323.
21. Oyler JM, Cone EJ, Joseph RE Jr, Huestis MA. Identification of hydrocodone in human urine following controlled codeine administration. J Anal Toxicol 2000; 24: 530–535.
22. Murao S, Manabe H, Yamashita T, Sekikawa T. Intoxication with over the counter antitussive medication containing dihydrocodeine and chlorpheniramine causes generalized convulsion and mixed acidosis. Intern Med 2008; 47: 1013–1015.
23. Coffman KL. The debate about marijuana usage in transplant candidates: recent medical evidence on marijuana health effects. Curr Opin Organ Transplant 2008; 13: 189–195.
24. Rossi S, Yasli T, Bentley H, van der Brande G et al. Characterization of interference with six commercial d9-tetrahydrocannabinol immunoassays by efavirenz glucuronide in urine. Clin Chem 2006; 52: 896–897 [letter to the Editor].
25. ElSohly MA, deWit H, Wachtel SR, Feng S et al. Delta 9-tetrahydrocannabivarin as a marker for ingestion of marijuana versus Marinol: results of a clinical study. J Anal Toxicol 2001; 25: 565–571.
26. di Tomaso E, Beltramo M, Piomelli D. Brain cannabinoids in chocolate. Nature 1996; 382(6593): 677–678.
27. James JS. Marijuana and chocolate. AIDS Treat News 1996; 18(2567): 3–4.
28. Tytgat J, Van Boven M, Daenens P. Cannabinoid mimics in chocolate utilized as an argument in court. Int J Legal Med 2000; 113: 137–139.

Subject Index

Note: The letters 'f' and 't' following locators refer to figures and tables respectively.

DOI 10.1007/978-1-60761-527-9,

Lightning Source UK Ltd.
Milton Keynes UK
16 September 2010

159917UK00006B/110/P

9 781607 615262